1

Awkward Silences and How to Prevent Them: 25 Tactics to Engage, Captivate, and Always Know What to Say

By Patrick King

Social Interaction Specialist and Conversation Coach
www.PatrickKingConsulting.com

Table of Contents

Introduction

I wish I could say that I'm immune to awkward silences, but that would be a huge lie.

I fall prey to them or create them just as much as anyone else. But I also know how to handle and recover from them seamlessly. The occasion that changed the way I view conversation and awkward silence occurred a few years ago and was eye-opening.

A friend of mine had just returned from what she described as a life-changing trip. It took her around the Middle East and lasted for about 60 days. She experienced how vastly different women were treated around the world, and saw firsthand the absurdly rich and the heartbreakingly impoverished—often on the same street.

You'd think I'd be incredibly fascinated to hear about her experiences and new insights, but I had just gotten a new job and was awash with a sense of self-importance and self-discovery. In hindsight, there probably wasn't going to be enough airspace for both of us to sufficiently speak, so there was either going to be a clash, or someone was going to have to sacrifice.

When we met for dinner, I didn't ask very many questions about her trip. I got a couple of stories out but, for the most part, kept bringing the conversation back to my new job and how it was affecting my life. The more I talked about myself, the more I noticed her mood shifting. *Awkward.*

When we first sat down, she was bursting at the seams to tell me about the intricacies of Middle Eastern cultures, but her mood became more and more sullen and withdrawn. We would constantly interrupt each other, trying to get a word in edgewise. *Awkward*.

The more I shared about myself, the better I felt, but that came at the cost of preventing her from doing the same. Every conversation, even between close friends, has limited airspace. I had polluted the airspace with statements and stories about me and prevented her from being able to do the same. We kept interrupting each other, and silence ensued as we slowly realized that we weren't getting what we wanted out of the conversation—to share and be validated. The conversation left us feeling unfulfilled and slightly annoyed. *Most definitely awkward*.

With the bad taste in my mouth remaining for the rest of the week, I was forced to re-examine how I approached others—and how people engaged in a general sense. What caused awkward silence or covert conflict? For most, a good conversation isn't necessarily about chemistry or flow—it's about being able to share and articulate their feelings and emotions. It's about the self-interest of allowing other people to see their inner greatness. It's about immersing yourself into a literally one-of-a-kind experience with others and letting go of preconceptions and judgments.

When you step over each other's toes, that's where the problems begin. Yes, we are all driven by self-interest and what we get out of a situation, even in our conversations with friends. Becoming conversationally great was about everything in moderation and balancing it all at once. I ended up calling my friend and asking her out to dinner again the next month, and wouldn't you know it—things went swimmingly because I shut my trap and just listened. After I did that for an hour, she did the same for me. *Awkwardness averted*.

This is a book about gaining friends and excelling in social situations. For some of you, that's going to entail fundamentally changing how you approach and engage with people. For others, it's going to be about avoiding the landmine of awkward silences and discovering how they form in the first place. Whatever the case, this book focuses on tactics and techniques to make you more interesting, emotionally in-tune, and easy to connect with.

Social awkwardness occurs because we're never trained how to think about interaction and keep it interesting. We typically see only one path that we're accustomed to, or we see zero paths because we are stuck in our heads, thinking about potential paths.

When you think of social awkwardness or awkward silences, chances are it causes a physical reaction—either from remembering a time you felt awkward, or when you couldn't wait to get away from someone else who was being awkward.

We know the feeling—it's similar to the tension of watching a scary movie and knowing that a ghost is going to pop onto screen soon. It's almost as if something fills the air that makes all the parties uncomfortable, with no clear way to go. In the midst of that confusion, no one says or does anything, and then the feeling just grows. Or that feeling just before you hit the top of the rollercoaster and start to plummet down. You just want to leave the situation prematurely instead of waiting for it to end naturally.

But what causes it in reality? There have been several studies attempting to put a label on this feeling that we all try to avoid on a daily basis.

Professor Joshua Clegg of John Jay College has been one of the most prominent researchers in the area of social awkwardness. He noted that there isn't still one single definition of feeling awkward—if you were to ask 100 people, you would probably get 100 different definitions and facial expressions. However, he framed it as a general violation of social norms and acting in a way that is incongruent and inappropriate for the current context. Sometimes, this behavior is *never* appropriate, such as staring at someone while licking your lips repeatedly.

Clegg proposed that the feeling of social awkwardness was a "social early warning system" that acted to protect people in social situations. In other words, when you noticed someone being socially awkward, you take note and pay special attention to them because it meant you might be more likely to suffer harm from them. When someone gives us odd feelings in any way, we are conditioned to move away and avoid them.

For instance, off-color jokes indicate that people aren't on the same wavelength and further aren't necessarily on the "normal" spectrum. If you don't understand social norms such as wiping your mouth or shaking hands, it leads people to wonder what other ways they will violate social boundaries. Staring too long or standing too close come with a lack of self-awareness that extends just how far?

In reality, it's easiest to think of social awkwardness as a lack of understanding of the unwritten manners and rules of social situations. There are universal rules, such as not staring at someone's lips and licking your own, but there are also context-dependent rules. You don't act the same at a funeral as you do at a party.

But just when you think you've mastered one set of rules, each conversation, interaction, group, and context has a different set of rules to learn. You can be completely socially fluent in one context and bumbling in another. The absence of learning these rules is what leads to your social awkwardness. It's the difference between how you act at a fine dining restaurant versus a hole-in-the-wall greasy spoon.

Manners and rules are important in society because they show respect and a willingness to cooperate with others. Many years ago, this could even mean they were a threat to your survival. Even something as small as someone neglecting to say thank-you could be seen as someone who might selfishly stray from the tribe. The simple truth is we are sensitive to those who deviate from the social constructs of our manners and rules.

There are obvious examples, but most of the situations you have to learn are far subtler. For instance, if you start at a new high school in a different country, you can't just come in guns blazing and expect to be the most popular kid there. Ideally, you would hang back and observe how kids might be different there first. Then, once you learn the lingo, unwritten rules, where all the different cliques hang out, and what kind of fashion is in, you'd be able to adapt and then finally make your move. At least, that's what you would do if you wanted social success. The socially awkward might disregard that and jump in like a bull in a China shop without regard to what might be different.

Simon Baron-Cohen of Oxford University found that people with the kinds of social skill deficits and communication problems that are stereotypical to awkward people tend to think in systematic, methodical ways. This style of thinking is well matched to tasks and occupations driven by logic (engineering, for instance), but is a terrible fit for social interactions, which are inherently unpredictable and lack structure and patterns. People can't be reduced to systems, and you can't run their actions through an algorithm.

Social awkwardness is like anything else—a habit and not a reflection of the underlying person. Just as some of us are less suited for geography, some of us are less suited for social interaction.

Pay attention to the different social rules presented in this book, as they'll become the systems you can follow. Accept that your goal is simply social calibration as opposed to overhauling your personality or fixing a fatal trait. You just need to know where to find where the unwritten social rules are inscribed, because they aren't where your customary ones are found.

Chapter 1. You Set the Tone

Most people don't barrel into conversation head-first. Rather, they gently slide in and test the waters. If you've never met someone before, you naturally feel like you need to feel them out and understand how they interact with people, and generally how loose and appropriate you can be.

For instance, remember when you were in elementary school and you found out you would have a substitute teacher the next day? It was a scary moment for most, unless you hated your normal teacher. It was scary because you never knew how strict or vicious the substitute would be, and you would have to be on your best behavior for a few days until you figured them out.

The next morning, suppose the substitute teacher walks in with impeccable posture and addresses everyone as "mister" and "miss" even though you are eight years old. That's the tone they chose to set, which is obviously not ideal for you. But what if the substitute teacher were to walk in with an untucked shirt and sandals, and immediately address the class as "buddies" and "dudes"? I'm not saying one is superior to the other, but a tone is clearly being set by each of these teachers.

In social conversations, people size you up in the same way. They look at how you carry yourself, and they are waiting for a sign that it's okay for them to be more relaxed and personable around you. In the vast majority of cases, they want to feel like you might with that second substitute teacher—they want signs they can relax and let their hair down, so to speak. You can set this tone with them.

Speak Like Children

One of the easiest ways to set a more casual and welcoming tone with others is to speak like a child might. What does that mean?

I had one of the most interesting conversations of the year a couple months ago, and you'll never guess who the other party was. Let me first tell you why exactly the conversation was so good. Predictably, I did most of the talking, as filling the air with your own voice is pretty gratifying.

This means that it wasn't particularly what my conversation partner said to me; it was the approach she had. My conversation partner essentially had no filter. This was refreshing, as most day-to-day banter can be uniform and vanilla. The lack of a filter means it will go places that are interesting, emotion-driven, and somewhat inappropriate.

Of course, the best topics are always inappropriate—very few topics are truly inappropriate, you just have to speak about those topics in an appropriate manner.

My conversation partner was also very direct and lacked any pretense or tact. They got straight to the point and any excuses or justifications I provided for my reasoning were shot down—some deservedly so. I could rationalize them to myself, but they didn't make sense to her, and she said it. Two plus two only equaled four, and nothing else could impact it. Speaking to someone who wasn't afraid of beating around the bush for the sake of social norms was refreshing. They weren't afraid of asking the deep and tough questions, no matter how often she had to ask, "But why?" to understand something. Often, it went down a hole that others would have avoided. She had to ask a few times before I readily admitted and opened up.

Finally, along with that lack of pretense for me was a lack of pretense for her. There was no judgment, and it was apparent that everything was motivated by sheer, genuine curiosity. It made me feel acceptable being vulnerable and sharing my more private thoughts.

You got me—the conversation partner was an eight-year-old I met at an acquaintance's barbeque. For most of us, we have trouble with conversation when we think about it too much. We analyze in our head, attempt to plan, and unnecessarily filter what we have to say. No matter how exciting or emotionally engaging the thoughts swimming around our noodle may be, what makes it out of our mouths can be downright dull. We stick to the tried and proven safe topics. We filter out the excitement and intrigue because we don't want to rile any feathers or because we are self-conscious ourselves.

Children do not have this problem, and that's the tone they set. This is always a choice you have as well.

They speak completely without filters and a lack of knowledge about what is socially acceptable and what is not. They spontaneously blurt out the first thing that comes to mind. I, for one, think that's a trait worth emulating. It makes people engaging, interesting, and, most of all, deep.

This is about shedding any preconceptions, judgments, assumptions, or filters and just speaking from the heart. Within reason, of course. When you can just be yourself without censorship, you will be a much more interesting person to speak with. And you can bet you will not be boring. Take a second and try to access your memory banks as to how you would have approached conversations as a child. You didn't have a filter, you showed emotions, and you said what was on your mind.

How can you speak more bravely and fearlessly?

First, children don't judge, and they have no preconceptions about how the world should be.

They don't cast judgment on you because they don't understand how to. This also means they don't feel judged or embarrassed for what they say. They don't think as much about what other people might think because they haven't been socialized to care. They just express whatever spontaneous thoughts come to mind.

This is much tougher for adults because by the time we grow up, we're a bundle of defensive nerves that have our guards constantly up from judgment and rejection. You don't need to suddenly grow immune to the fear of judgment, but it's important to realize that's why you don't open your mouth sometimes. It's not necessarily a problem that you don't have anything to say. The problem is actually that you don't feel comfortable with anything you'd actually want to say.

Here's what you do know: the broad parameters of what's acceptable topic-wise. All you need to do to start speaking in a freer, more child-like manner is to deviate outside of those bounds 1% at a time. It may be only 1%, but it will be exponentially more entertaining and interesting for all involved parties. People do judge, but not nearly as much as you think. It is only in your mind that the spotlight is constantly on you.

Second, children think literally.

Children don't use metaphor or analogy. They lack the cognitive capacity. They must rely on literal descriptions and combinations of concepts from their world to call the world as they see it. New concepts are either completely foreign, or combinations of concepts they are already familiar with. For instance, a tall man looks like "a man but he is walking in mommy's high-heeled shoes."

Interestingly enough, this is exactly why so many comedians are funny. Their humor is rooted in the raw level of honesty of their everyday observations and descriptions. For example, a butt looks like "two Pringles hugging," or proclaiming that "Vapor rub is spicy" or "a car looks like a lampshade." They make the familiar appear new and unexpected, and that is one of the cornerstones of humor.

As long as you make sure you're not overly offensive, these types of statements based on literal observations and descriptions will bring a new level of discussion. They also show insight because people might otherwise miss it. Too often they're thinking in metaphors or analogies, or "higher level" thinking. When you get down to the basics and describe things on as simple of a level as possible, people appreciate it.

Third, children show raw emotion without filters.

Whenever I'm in a public space and a child is throwing a tantrum to their parent, I feel deep pity for the parent. They are in a lose-lose situation—they can't discipline the child in public, but they also can't very well just cave in to the child's demands.

Children show emotion without filtering themselves whatsoever. You don't have to show this amount of emotion, but you also don't have to suppress your true emotions like you probably are.

It shows genuineness, honesty, transparency, and vulnerability. When you show your raw emotions, especially emotions that make you appear vulnerable, people will immediately grow more comfortable with you. Why is that? Because you have shown yourself to be expressive and honest. That makes you trustworthy, dependable, and predictable in a good way. People know what they're getting with you and feel like you're not hiding anything.

People (adults) are usually trying to be something or someone they're not, trying to sound a certain way, or trying to achieve an ulterior motive of some sort. It's essentially normalized dishonesty on a daily basis. Children just express what they're feeling as they're feeling it. You might think expressing your raw emotions creates tension in others; it can if you throw a tantrum. But allowing others to view and even participate in your emotional state is a huge connecting experience.

Fourth, children will "go there."

They haven't quite developed the self-awareness to know when they are offending people. Have you ever been around a child when someone with a birth defect walks by? The child will usually be mystified and fascinated, staring with impunity.

They are not shy and aren't afraid to keep asking questions, despite the rabbit hole they might slither down. They just don't know better and want a satisfactory answer to their questions and curiosity. They don't care about the "appropriateness" adults get hung up on.

The reason most adults pull back is because we feel embarrassed or we're afraid of making the other person feel embarrassed. The vast majority of the time, our fears are unjustified. The worst part is that because we hold back, we don't ask the interesting questions that could actually take the conversation to a much higher—and more interesting—level.

Children, on the other hand, just dig and dig some more, and they keep on digging. You might want to try this yourself. Keep in mind that there's a big difference between digging by asking question after question and asking the same question over and over again. If you ask the same question over and over again, you're being annoying. When you keep digging out of seemingly genuine curiosity, you further the conversation.

Children speak with utmost freedom, and there's nothing stopping you from this as well.

Intellectualize Less

Speaking like children sets a more casual and open tone—that's something you should actively do.

Something you should actively avoid is to intellectualize conversations. Of course, children don't do that either. There are many ways you can categorize or label conversations. One major method is to split conversations into the categories of "emotional" and "intellectual."

Emotional interactions are based on feelings, experiences, hopes, and dreams, and they are inherently personal. This is how you engage with friends and family and people you actually care about. Intellectual interactions, on the other hand, are based on ideas, technical details, and simple information exchange. This is what an interview sounds like most of the time.

We all frequently use both, but which do you think you should embody more when you want to connect with another human being? They have very different uses.

Intellectual interactions, as mentioned, are about exchanging information. This means one or both parties are learning, discussing, or debating. This is when a professor lectures or you work with a friend to plan a trip. This is also when you ask questions about someone's background and how they like their job. You might imagine that most conversations that occur in the workplace are information exchanges by nature. This is an easier way to interact, so we slip into this mode more often than not without realizing it.

These are important functions, but they aren't necessarily the most conducive to socializing. By contrast, what does an emotional conversation sound like?

It's when you discuss how you feel about events in your life, your current struggles and triumphs, and what shared emotions you might have. This is where intimacy is able to take root and thrive. This is when you talk about a recent relationship breakup and how sad it makes you. This is where you discuss how you both feel similarly about the fact that your parents are aging. It also might be how you talk about your feelings about your job, instead of your actual job duties. Ask how people feel about something rather than how it went or what they did.

Intellectual conversations create the feeling that you are filling out a survey for an insurance company, whereas emotional conversations are what you have with your close friends. Emotions are universal, while experiences and dry details are not.

You can either discuss how and when you visited your grandparents, or how it made you feel. Again, there are clear occasions when intellectual conversations make the most sense. But are you making the mistake of applying that level of analysis and data collection to your social conversations?

Just like with child-like speaking, you are always presented with the choice on how to set the tone of your interaction. You can hold back, or you can speak more child-like. You can intellectualize, or you can speak emotionally. Obviously, these aren't the only dimensions upon which you can choose, but it is *you* choosing every time. You want to be the proverbial teacher who walks in, swears, and makes the entire class breathe a sigh of relief and relax.

Chapter 2. The Devil Is in the Details

If you were to buy a brand-new camera, you might think that it has pretty good resolution and does a great job of capturing everything it should. Every person, face, and even ceiling tile will make it into the picture in more detail than you could ever imagine. You can even zoom in and see someone's nose hairs that they have recently trimmed.

But even this type of attention doesn't compare to the details that our subconscious captures about other people. For instance, have you ever felt that you just didn't have chemistry with someone, or you just didn't like their "vibe"? Something about them felt off?

This means that your brain was subconsciously tracking them, and took notice of something that was either inconsistent or negative. Consciously, they may have been generous and kind to your face, but since your brain has the benefit of your entire life of experience, plus hundreds of thousands of years of evolution, it's designed to see patterns that elude us at face value.

Thus, the devil is in the details in how you present yourself. One misstep can lead to the dreaded awkward silence, and it might not matter how consciously nice or generous you are. You *know* you should be kind and listen to others, but these are the big things you should take care of. This chapter is devoted to the little things that matter that you may never have even thought about. You don't know what you don't know!

Upspeak

If you're not familiar with upspeak, I'll paint you a picture. You are asking someone what time a movie begins, and they reply. The only thing is, their reply takes the form of a question rather than an answer in tone.

A: What time does the movie start?
B: 7:00 at night?
A: Are you sure about that?

Does this person actually know the answer, are they lying to you, or are they just confused? Imagine this tone of uncertainty and lack of confidence in every reply. For those of you who have seen that infamous scene in the movie *Anchorman* where Ron Burgundy reads a teleprompter saying, "I'm Ron Burgundy . . . ?" That's all upspeak.

Upspeak, occasionally known as uptalk, is when you phrase your declarative sentences as questions. Doing this doesn't follow expected speech patterns to others, so it causes confusion and misinterpretation all around. To put it more tangibly, upspeak occurs when your vocal intonation rises at the end of a sentence—that rising intonation is what normally indicates a question.

What's your favorite restaurant?
[That is a real question.]

Burger King?
[Is that your final answer?]

The lilt or rise in tone at the end of this sentence turns what should be an answer into a question, making it seem as if you are not sure. You may start noticing this more with your friends and acquaintances, and studies show it happens more often with female speakers. Why is this a problematic habit?

Most people are deathly afraid of confrontation on a daily basis. Some of us are okay with it, and there is a fraction of people who actively seek it out. Upspeak is a subtle way to avoid confrontation and accommodate right off the bat. It's used to ask for acceptance and show a willingness to change their declared intent, even if that's not really what they want.

The problem is, more often than not, using upspeak doesn't create the impression of any of those things. It just serves to make you sound unsure, passive, unconfident, and as if you don't know what you're talking about. The more official and regulated the environment, the worse it makes you sound.

A: Johnson, was your analysis on those files accurate?
B: Yes . . . ?
A: Wait . . . Do you even know what I'm talking about?

By using upspeak, you appear afraid. You sound tentative. You sound confused and noncommittal. You're testing the waters to make sure what you're saying is acceptable. You're looking for validation. You're allowing what you think others want to hear to influence what you say. It can have a very real impact on your job and career.

Imagine how upspeak will make you appear in front of a client, coworker, supervisor, or manager. You create an indecisive, unconfident, and insecure impression, as if you have no clue about what you're talking about. If someone asks your opinion on some work analyses, they want assurance that you've (1) actually done it, and (2) have an opinion about it. Upspeak eliminates both from the table—along with your credibility.

This is even more important when you're in a leadership position. You will be expected to be assertive and certain and have justifications for your decisions. Your statements should inspire confidence in others; using upspeak will put each statement you make under heavy scrutiny. You should be giving instructions and inspiration but instead you'll end up appearing as if you're just looking for approval from subordinates.

In a social setting, or when you're surrounded by friends and family, upspeak is a lesser offense. After all, these are the people you care about, so they might not mind repeating themselves in lieu of receiving information. Sometimes it's just a discussion or debate, so you actually need to hedge statements to make sure you're not offending anyone and allowing wiggle room. However, it's still going to be occasionally frustrating for your friends to deal with because upspeak puts the burden of decision- and plan-making onto other people. Essentially, this is when you ask someone what they want to eat, and they always reply with, "I don't know. What do *you* want to eat?"

By the way, another subtle way you might be defaulting to upspeak is if your sentences constantly trail off instead of end in a declarative way. For example, "Yeah, let's go bowling …"

Perhaps the worst unintended consequence is that you actively make other people uneasy and uncomfortable because it appears to them you are hiding your true intentions. That's what happens when there is inconsistency between your words, your tone, and your actions. Others will feel as if they can't read you or what you want, and they won't relax around you because they won't be sure about how you will respond. It would be like if someone simultaneously invited you to dinner while frowning and shaking their head. Who knows how genuine their invitation is.

If you're tempted to use upspeak to hedge your bets, just keep this one rule in mind. When people ask you questions, they just want an answer. They don't want to have to interpret you, your words, or your intent. They want real, direct, helpful information that they can respond to—not to repeat their question multiple times before receiving any.

So now that you're aware of what upspeak is and how it might be subtly sabotaging your attempts at connecting with others, how can you address it?

First, be clear and conscious as to whether you actually mean to ask a question, or you want to make a statement. While the thoughts are still forming in the wrinkles of your brain, take a definitive stance on whether you are asking or stating. If you are asking, then ask the question directly. Don't answer it. If you are stating, don't use upspeak because it will undermine the intent of your words. As I mentioned, it can be very frustrating for others if they never feel as if they know what you truly mean or want.

Second, practice ending your statements with a declarative tone.

A declarative tone decreases at the end of a statement, and slightly emphasizes the last word to make it clear that you are asserting something. It leaves no room for question or doubt. Try saying the following sentence out loud first as a question and then as a statement. Notice the difference in rising and falling tones at the end?

I'm going to eat a sandwich and I will see you later.

Upspeak occurs because you are really trying to determine whether something is acceptable or okay. You're not entirely comfortable and you are afraid of rejection.

You don't want to look stupid by being immediately contradicted or wrong. Thus, upspeak is an abbreviated way of asking that question.

Upspeak abbreviation: *I'm going to eat a sandwich and I will see you later?*

The uncut version: *I'm going to eat a sandwich and I will see you later.* <u>*How does that sound, and is it acceptable for you?*</u>

Upspeak is a habit many of us have been socialized with since we were very young. It will take practice to rectify this problem, but this small but consequential change can greatly affect the way you are perceived by others, and in turn the way you feel about yourself.

Time Limits

Human attention spans are far worse than you could ever imagine. That's why TED Talks are capped at 18 minutes, and it's why movies are rarely longer than 2.5 hours (John

Medina). It's because people can't pay attention that long, no matter how riveted they are. The brain gets fatigued, and has to either take a break to indulge in a distraction to recharge and be able to function once more.

TED Talks are more active, participatory, and dense; thus, they must be shorter. Movies are more passive and visual; thus, they can be longer. This is right in line with additional studies that show the attention span of healthy adults to be, on average, right around 15 minutes. Conversations, of course, are exponentially more participatory than a TED Talk, so adjust the attention span accordingly again.

What does this have to do with conversations? There are two main takeaways from understanding how human attention spans work.

First, this should inform you as to the natural and optimal length of a conversation. Of course, we can talk to our friends for hours, but those are not the conversations you need help with, are they? With strangers and people you meet at networking events, interest just may start to wane around the 15-minute mark. And that's okay as long as you are prepared for it and expect it.

This means you should strive to make your impact and personality felt as soon as possible—because people have the natural tendency to grow bored or fatigued within minutes. Longer conversations are obviously positive, but think of the 15-minute mark as your threshold for whether you should stay or disengage. If it's still lukewarm at that point, it's only going to get worse because people's attention spans will have melted away.

Second, if human attention spans are so short, it means you should necessarily limit the amount of consecutive speaking you do. In other words, a conversation is not a lecture or speech, so you shouldn't at any point find yourself speaking for longer than 30 seconds at a time. One of the biggest conversational failings is the inability to recognize when someone is no longer listening to you. It's mostly because we are far too interested in ourselves that we don't notice when people's eyes glaze over or start wandering through the room behind us.

Combine our short attention spans with the knowledge that short-term memory is only equipped to hold seven items at once and you quickly come to the realization that you should probably shut up more often. If you're trying to argue a point, you can't list them out verbally like bullet points because people literally won't remember them, and will likely only reply to either the first or the last point you make.

It also means your stories are probably too long and include details people won't care about or remember. Downsize your story lengths to make them more impactful and keep people's attention. Alternatively, you can pace yourself better and make sure exciting points of your story come out at least every 30 seconds. Don't take it personally; people just aren't wired to pay close attention to one thing for an extended period of time. If you make the assumption that people's attention spans are limited, constantly waning, and fragile, you will value them more and engage in a completely different manner.

You know how easy it is for people to cave to the impulse of pulling their phones out. It's usually a sign that you've failed in one way or another. You have to captivate and get to the point as quickly as possible. And yet still, if you catch yourself speaking for 25 seconds, chances are that someone is bored somewhere. Cater to this and you will have far fewer awkward silences and conversations that seem to run out of steam prematurely.

This isn't even mentioning that you should ask more questions than you answer to keep people engaged, but that's a point to be made repeatedly throughout this book.

Linguistic Choices

Just like the slight tone of upspeak can make a big difference in how people perceive you, so can small linguistic choices. The words and phrases we use aren't as universal as we think—everyone has their own interpretation behind the everyday words we all use.

This goes back to the existential question, is my concept of green everyone else's concept of green? Or do others perceive as blue what I perceive as green?

The point is, the words we use, no matter how carefully we choose them, have the potential to offend someone out there. With this in mind, one of the ways to prevent this to a certain degree is presented by Alfred Korzybski, a scholar who developed a field called *general semantics*. He posited that we should strive to remove "to be" verbs such as "I am," "she is," "they are," and "we are" from our daily usage.

Why would you ever want to do that? Well, Korzybski's reasoning was rooted in the fact that using "to be" verbs creates inaccurate statements. For instance, "I am an idiot" isn't true. The sentiment that is actually meant to be expressed is, "I feel like an idiot because I did something an idiot might do." So from a factual standpoint, using these types of verbs is incorrect. But the rest of us care about such pedantry, so why does it really matter?

Using these types of verbs makes you sound overly judgmental even if you don't mean to be. For instance, in an argument, is there a difference between saying, "You are such an idiot" and "You did such an idiotic thing"?

The first is a personal insult that will probably cause massive defensiveness. The second, however, is about their actions and not them as a person. It may still cause defensiveness, but it's much easier to admit that you did something dumb versus admitting you are a dumb person. You can see how big a difference omitting these verbs and being specific with your real intent can make.

What about the following?

"I'm a failure" versus "I failed yesterday."

"They are insensitive" versus "They were insensitive in reaction to that one event."

The first statements are overgeneralizations that may or may not be fair. There is a lack of nuance, and they are statements that create self-fulfilling prophecies and negative self-esteem. The second statements are more nuanced while keeping the people themselves untouched. It's not likely that people will notice when you remove the verbs, but they will definitely notice when you keep them in and lay judgment upon them!

Another way small linguistic tweak that can make a difference in how people perceive you is knowledge of the words that people really pay attention to. You can call them power words or whatever you want, but they are words that literally make people's brains activate in different ways (Gregory Ciotti).

Ready for the words?

1. You

2. Free
3. Because
4. Instantly
5. New

Let's dive into why these words are so impactful, and how you can adapt their sentiment to everyday life.

You—This can be summed up by this famous Dale Carnegie quote, "Remember that a person's name is to that person the sweetest and most important sound in any language." There's a little more to it, though. We become engaged when people appeal to us specifically because it makes us feel like we are being catered to and, for lack of a better word, special. I like feeling special, don't you? To make more use of this, use people's names in daily conversation more, especially when you want to emphasize a point or bring their attention to something specific.

Free—This instantly grabs people's attention because everyone loves free things.

Personally, I will gladly accept a terrible pizza if it's free. We like getting value from nothing, and we also have a natural tendency toward the concept of *loss aversion*, which means that we hate to miss out on things or not maximize them. To make use of this knowledge, frame your conversation topic in terms of the benefit they are getting out of it—whether it be pleasure, fun, information, advice, or help. This will make people fulfill their loss aversion tendencies.

Because—This word is powerful because it brings people to the payoff they are likely waiting for. It prefaces the juicy part of any story, because the justification and reasons are more compelling to hear about. On a broader level, famed psychologist Robert Cialdini found that using the word "because" massively skyrocketed compliance with requests for no reason other than people liked having reasons for their actions. Whether it's a story, or making a request of someone, using "because" will engage people more. To make use of this knowledge, always provide a reason, even if it is flimsy or obvious.

Instantly—Humans are in the business of immediate gratification and pleasure. If I want something, I want it yesterday and don't want to wait for it. When we hear the word "instantly" or words similar in tenor, we literally perk up because we start to anticipate the next action. It makes it feel like something will occur, well, instantly, so people can't help but be engaged for the next few moments. To make use of this knowledge, think about how movies do it. They create cliffhangers and motion out of nothing. Talk about action in terms of how quickly and surprisingly it occurred, and how imminent the impact will be.

New—Human brains are also suckers for novelty. When we are exposed to something we are unfamiliar with, we are either skeptical or curious. Either reaction is more engaged than when we are exposed to known quantities. There may not be inherent trust, but there is inherent will to investigate and discover. It's much easier to talk to people about something that is new and exciting versus tired and old. To make use of this information, start describing your views, interests, stories, and hobbies as new experiences or discoveries to differentiate them.

As the chapter title states, the devil is always in the detail. These were just a few of the subconscious tics that humans don't consciously perceive, but have been shown to respond to consistently. Your tone of voice in avoiding upspeak is important because it's part of your overall body language and how people perceive you. What's just as important is the knowledge of our short attention spans, meaning you should strive to make immediate impact. Finally, words and phrases matter more than you might think, as demonstrated by Korzybski's verbs and Ciotti's overall findings about power words.

Chapter 3. HPM + SBR

HPM and SBR sitting in a tree. K-I-S-S-I-N-G?

Not quite. Something that tends to create awkward silence is when people run out of things to say. Of course, this isn't usually the problem where people literally have nothing to say on a matter or topic. It's usually a problem of not feeling comfortable enough to say what's on their mind, and thus they can't think of anything to say that they feel is properly filtered.

Here, I want to introduce six extremely effective types of responses for just about anything. This is important because, as you know, our minds go blank sometimes. Therefore, having six types of responses you can literally go down the list with has some value.

HPM

HPM is one of my favorite conversation tactics because I believe it is so widely applicable.

It stands for History, Philosophy, and Metaphor.

History is your personal experience and memories about the topic at hand. Everyone has memories, even if they have to borrow memories of other people. Imagine the key phrase as *I remember when I …*

Philosophy is your personal feelings, stance, or opinion on the topic at hand. Everyone has personal feelings, again, even if they have to borrow from someone else. Imagine the key phrase as *I really love/hate that because …*

Finally, Metaphor is an external topic, related or not, that the topic at hand reminds you of. Everyone can create metaphors; it's just a matter of practicing your sense of imagination. Imagine the key phrase as *That totally makes me think of …*

The very point of HPM is that everyone has an H, P, and M. The reason I feel it is widely applicable is because everyone has these things in their life. You have memories, you have opinions, and you likely can make connections if you bother to think about them—so knowing about HPM is almost like having cue cards right in front of you while you are immersed in a conversation or stuck in an awkward silence.

All you need to do is think HPM when you're faced with a pending silence and you'll have something to say.

There will always be awkward spots in any conversation. It doesn't matter whether you're the best conversationalist in the world. There will always be those times when conversation dwindles away or there is dead air. By knowing HPM, you increase the likelihood that awkward spots won't be noticeable at all.

Let's put HPM into action with a topic you feel you have nothing to say about. For me, this would be something like NASCAR (car racing). After all, I live in San Francisco, and the mediocre public transportation system is what the vast majority of people use to get around here.

Suppose someone brings up their love of NASCAR, which I know almost nothing about. My HPM would go like this:

History: I've never been to a NASCAR event, but they look incredible. One of my friends said it was unexpectedly thrilling. Have you been to many? [My lack of personal history and drawing on someone else's history regarding NASCAR.]

Philosophy: NASCAR events look amazingly fun. I feel that it's something you have to be in the stadium for. It's got to be more than just sitting and watching the cars, right? [Asserting an opinion about NASCAR events.]

Metaphor: Those NASCAR cars always have lots of sponsors, right? Reminds me of European soccer teams and their uniforms. Crazy! [Took an element of the topic and related it to something entirely different.]

Let's try it with another topic so you get the hang of it a bit better. I wish I would tell you to pick one at random, but I will again: dinosaurs. Someone brings up their love of dinosaurs upon seeing graffiti on the walls.

History: My favorite movie of all time is actually *Jurassic Park*, so me too. I remember the first time I watched it. I couldn't sleep for a few days.

Philosophy: I love dinosaurs, too. My favorite is the mild triceratops. Which is yours?

Metaphor: Dinosaurs remind me of our friend Jim. They have the same body structure, right?

While HPM is great, it doesn't resonate with everyone. There are a couple of aspects to note. First, it's all about you. This can be good or bad. If you feel you need to share more about yourself, then it's great. However, if you find that you constantly insert your own stories into the conversation, it's not so great.

Second, HPM requires you to draw internally and determine what you think about something, or access something from your memory banks. It can be difficult to generate original thoughts and statements without practice, and can take many of us out of the moment completely. HPM is completely user-generated, instead of building upon something else from the conversation. Thankfully, SBR is the complete opposite. HPM draws internally, but SBR draws externally.

SBR

SBR stands for Specific, Broad, and Related. This means you work with the exact topic that is given, and make statements or ask questions about it in a specific, broad, or related manner. For many people, this is easier because it allows them to just work in the moment and react to the last thing that was said to them. You can be more of a parrot when you use SBR.

SBR is a great conversation device because it's contextual. It doesn't require reaching into your memory banks or expertise the way HPM does. SBR sticks to the topics that you're already talking about and manipulates or repositions them so you can remain on topic. In some cases, you may have hit a point in the conversation where HPM is unavailable or just doesn't make sense for you. In those cases, you can quickly snap into SBR.

Here's how SBR works.

S stands for Specific. This is when you ask a question or make a statement that goes deeper and more in-depth about the topic at hand.

For example, if someone is talking about building cars, you might ask questions like, "So then what happens when you build it this way?" or "I've never heard of someone doing that. How long does that take exactly, and what tools do you need?"

Even if you don't know anything about the topic, and sometimes especially when you don't know anything about the topic, bounce it back to the person speaking so you can learn more. Give the other person the spotlight and allow them to get into the nitty gritty details. Ask for them. When you get specific, you also inevitably touch upon people's thought processes and motivations, something people typically love to share.

If they are building something, try to find out how it works and why they are doing it. Try to gain enough knowledge such that you could build it yourself at some point. Act as if you are really trying to gain a deep understanding of what is happening in the topic.

Why questions are good here. *Who, what, when,* and *where* questions work better in the next category.

B stands for Broad. This is when you ask a question or make a statement that is more general to the topic at hand. Where before you zoomed in, here you are zooming out.

As mentioned, if someone is telling you about how they are building a car, you can ask *who, what, when,* and *where* questions. Who did you build it with? What kind of car was it? When was this? Where did you keep the parts?

Broad questions take a step back and collect the context and background of a topic, which might be necessary to being able to understand the topic at all. You aren't necessarily changing topics, but you are seeing what topics are interrelated with the one you are zooming away from. If someone tells you about their ski trip, zooming out would be to discover the context of the trip, where they went, whom they went with, and what happened. You are trying to understand the topic from a bird's eye view.

R stands for Related. If you can't think of anything specific or broad to say, you can find a topic related to the topic at hand. This is similar to the metaphor portion of HPM because the questions are somewhat alike. Remember the key phrase there—*That makes me think of ...*

For example, if the topic at hand is building cars, you don't need to ask more about it if you flat out don't care. Just take a tiny element, however related or unrelated, and use it to bring up a different topic. Use it as a springboard or launching pad.

Building cars makes me think of the gym ... It's such hard work, right?

Building cars reminds me of building my computer. Have you done that before?

Just as easy as *cat* makes you think of *dog*, there are similar reactions to other words and topics.

Pencils? Related to school.
Coffee? Related to Starbucks.
Pineapple? Related to Hawaii or certain hairstyles.
Ceramics? Related to that one sexy scene in the movie *Ghost*.

SBR is a powerful conversation device because it allows you to stay in the moment and yet never run out of things to say. You won't fall into the common pitfall of trying to be present and in the moment AND trying to think about what you are going to say next. Unfortunately, most people's brains cannot do two things at once, so that is doomed to failure.

SBR lets you appear curious and engaged in the conversation, which creates the comfort necessary for rapport. You will naturally be asking more questions and focusing on the other person, which tends to build balance and make the other person happy in general.

If there's a pitfall with SBR, it's focusing on one category too much. If you ask too many specific questions, you risk the conversation becoming too technical with nowhere to go. If it becomes too technical, it will become hard for you to understand and care about. The other person will likely notice your disinterest and will feel as if you are tuning them out. It creates a cycle.

And of course, if you ask too many broad questions, you can bore the other person. This means you will be asking about the context and background—nothing substantive—and jumping from topic to topic. That sounds like the kind of small talk that people love to hate.

Finally, the downside to asking too many R questions is that it makes you look as if you can't focus on anything or are perpetually distracted. It's like you keep seeing shiny objects and changing your mind based on them. It also makes it seem as if you don't care about their answers because you are immediately steering away into a different topic. This is also reminiscent of the small talk that makes networking events a nightmare for most.

Your Patterns

Optimally, you want to be able to switch between the three categories of SBR as well as the three categories in HPM. It requires practice, and the first step is to adequately understand and master each of the six types of responses.

Once you start playing with them, patterns will start to emerge with the types of statements that come most naturally to you. We all tend to engage in specific patterns, whether we realize it or not.

Do you tend to talk more about yourself or ask questions? Are you more externally focused and present, or more in your head during conversations? Do you enjoy talk about emotions or abhor them? Do you have a bad memory that renders you useless in talking about your personal experiences?

No one can answer these questions but you. But you'll find that a few of these six response types will resonate better than the others. My pattern is a combination of History, Specific, and Related—HSR. It's just how I tend to approach and think about the world, as well as the people in it. This means I am more interested in asking questions and understand others versus sharing about myself.

Which spring most readily to *your* mind? Pick three. These are your fallback go-tos. And start working on the other three, because having all of them in your pocket will make you that much better and versatile of a conversationalist.

Chapter 4. Tell Me a Story

You've probably read a good amount of content about how to be a good storyteller.

Some of these pieces of advice will reference Joseph Campbell, Homer (of *The Iliad* fame), and Steven Spielberg. Others will tell you that your story must have a beginning, middle, and ending. Let's see, what else is there? Oh, there's probably a bit about having a main character and action, or how you have to be as descriptive as possible so as to draw people into their imaginations.

These are all helpful to varying degrees, but they are about telling stories and taking the spotlight.

Very rarely are you taught how to elicit, listen to, and react to the stories of other people. After all, there are at least two people in a conversation, and you absolutely shouldn't be the only one that ends up telling stories. In fact, if you find yourself in that role, it might not be because your stories are inherently thrilling, or you're even a good storyteller. It might just be because you don't listen well to the stories of others, you stifle them, and then you subject people to yourself.

In any case, learning to listen well and elicit a productive response is a handy skill to have. In this chapter, there are some surprising methods to show that you're present and interested. Again, we know the basics that we should try to avoid one-word answers and always ask for more, but there are a few turns of phrase that make people want to open up to you—sometimes to a degree you might not even want. Overall, this chapter teaches you how to assist people in becoming great storytellers themselves.

Once you're on the listener side of the spectrum, you will necessarily learn how to stay and keep engaged when you're on the storytelling side as well.

Ask for a Story

When you watch sports, one of the most illogical parts is the post-game or post-match interview. These athletes are still caught in the throes of adrenaline, out of breath, and occasionally drip sweaters onto the reporters.

Yet when you are watching a broadcaster interview an athlete, does anything odd strike you about the questions they ask? The interviewers are put into an impossible situation and usually walk away with decent soundbites—at the very least, not audio disasters. Their duty is to elicit a coherent answer from someone who is mentally incoherent at the moment. How do they do that?

They'll ask questions like, "So tell me about that moment in the second quarter. What did you feel about it and how did the coach turn it around then?" as opposed to "How'd you guys win?" or "How did you turn this match around, comeback, and pull out all the stops to grab the victory at the very end?" as opposed to "How was the comeback?"

The key? They ask for a story rather than an answer. They phrase their inquiry in a way that can only be answered with a story, in fact.

Detail, context, and boundaries are given for the athletes to set them up to talk as much as possible instead of providing a breathless one-word answer. It's almost as if they provide the athletes with an outline of what they want to hear and how they can proceed. They make it easy for them to tell a story and simply engage. It's like if someone asks you a question but, in the question, tells you exactly what they want to hear as hints.

Sometimes we think we are doing the heavy lifting in a conversation and the other party isn't giving us much to work with. But that's a massive cop-out. They might not be giving you much, but you also might be asking them the wrong questions, which is making them give you terrible responses. In fact, if you think you are shouldering the burden, you are definitely asking the wrong questions.

Conversation can be much more pleasant for everyone involved if you provide fertile ground for people to work in. Don't set the other person up to fail and be a poor conversationalist; that will only make you invest and care less and cause the conversation to die out.

When people ask me low-effort, vague questions, I know they probably aren't interested in the answer. They're just filling the time and silence. To create win-win conversations and better circumstances for all, ask for stories the way the sports broadcasters do. Ask questions in a way that makes people want to share.

Stories are personal, emotional, and compelling. There is a thought process and narrative that necessarily exists. They are what show your personality, and how you can learn about someone. They show people's emotions and how they think. Last but not least, they show what you care about.

Compare this with simply asking for close-ended answers. Answers are often too boring and routine for people to care. They will still answer your questions, but in a very literal way, and the level of engagement won't be there. Peppering people with shallow questions puts people in a position to fail conversationally.

It's the difference between asking, "What was the best part of your day so far? Tell me how you got that parking space so close!" instead of just, "How are you?"

When you ask somebody the second question, you're asking for a quick, uninvolved answer. When you ask somebody one of the first two questions, you're inviting them to tell a specific story about their day. You are inviting them to narrate the series of events that made their day great or not. And it can't really be answered with a one-word answer.

Another example is, "What is the most exciting part of your job? How does it feel to make a difference like that?" instead of simply asking them the generic, "What do you do?" When you only ask somebody what they do for a living, you know exactly how the rest of the conversation will go: "Oh, I do X. What about you?"

A final example is, "How did you feel about your weekend? What was the best part? It was so nice outside" instead of just, "How was your weekend?"

Prompting others for stories instead of simple answers gives them a chance to speak in such a way that they feel emotionally invested. This increases the sense of meaning they get from the conversation you're having with them. It also makes them feel you are genuinely interested in hearing their answer because your question doesn't sound generic.

Consider the following guidelines when asking a question:

1. Ask for a story
2. Be broad, but with specific directions or prompts
3. Ask about feelings and emotions
4. Give the other person a direction to expand their answer into, and give them multiple prompts, hints, and possibilities
5. If all else fails, directly ask, "Tell me the story about …"

Imagine that you want the other person to inform your curiosity. Other examples include the following:

1. "Tell me about the time you …" versus "How was that?"
2. "Did you like that …" versus "How was it?"
3. "You look focused. What happened in your morning …" versus "How are you?"

Let's think about what happens when you elicit (and provide) personal stories instead of the old, tired automatic replies.

You say hello to your coworker on Monday morning and you ask how his weekend was. At this point, you have cataloged what you will say in case he asks you the same. Remember, they probably don't care about the actual answer ("good" or "okay"), but they *would* like to hear something interesting. But you never get the chance, because you ask him, "How was your weekend? Tell me about the most interesting part—I know you didn't just watch a movie at home!"

He opens up and begins to tell you about his Saturday night when he separately and involuntarily visited a strip joint, a funeral, and a child's birthday party. That's a conversation that can take off and get interesting, and you've successfully bypassed the unnecessary and boring small talk that plagues so many of us.

Most people love talking about themselves. Use this fact to your advantage. Once someone takes your cue and starts sharing a story, make sure you are aware of how you're responding to that person through your facial expressions, gestures, body language, and other nonverbal signals. Since there is always at least one exciting thing in any story, focus on that exciting point and don't be afraid to show that you're engaged.

Make Others the Hero

Remember the story from the introduction? I had a similar occurrence much more recently when I was able to schedule a lunch with one of my oldest friends.

The lunch did not go as planned. I had just returned from six months of mostly being on the road for one reason or another, and his only acknowledgment that I had even been gone was his sole question at the beginning of lunch: "So how was your trip?"

I told him my emotions, mentality, and related a couple of stories to showcase some of the unique things I experienced. He nodded and smiled. And then he turned the conversation to himself, his workplace drama, and how long his commute had gotten. I had learned my lesson the first time, so I directed the conversation to what he wanted to discuss.

I realize that he might have just been disinterested in my travels, but that's not the point. We're never 100% invested and engaged in what is important to other people, but that doesn't mean we can just pivot topics and completely ignore what the other person brings to the table.

That's what I mean by making others the hero—the hero of the conversation, the hero of their stories, and the main topic of discussion. If we're not careful, we often default to becoming the heroes of all of our conversations and stories. The other person necessarily becomes the supporting actor, and this can be frustrating and tiring to keep saying things like, "Oh wow, that's cool. Sounds so interesting. Whoa!"

People enjoy sharing about themselves and talking about their lives and thoughts. People also feel that a conversation goes poorly if they don't have that opportunity. By constantly making yourself the hero, you're denying people that chance and, by default, making their conversations poor.

If you lack the social self-awareness to know that you are dominating a conversation, you will quickly turn into "that guy" or "that girl" that people avoid because you talk their ears off about yourself.

I recall one specific instance at a networking event I was attending where I happened to be speaking with the ultimate "that girl." I was extremely disinterested in what she was saying because it was 100% about her, without my asking or prompting. At some point, I decided to see if she'd notice my blatant signs of disinterest, and the answer was a resounding no. At one point I was turned around completely and looking around the room and she was still talking to me. She definitely fought to be the hero in that conversation, and it was definitely one-sided.

A good litmus test of whether you are guilty of this is how much you know about your friends and acquaintances. When you engage others, do you ask how they're doing? And when you ask, are you listening to what they're saying and asking further? Do you care, or are you just waiting for your turn to speak?

Do you know much about your coworkers other than you share the same space and same coffee maker? Or would you say that they know much more about you because you don't ask or care about their lives? Do you actually have an interest and curiosity in the other person's life?

Do you consider it a waste of time to engage others and just want to share yourself? Do you know more about them, or do they know vastly more about you? If you know nothing about them, I've got bad news. Adjustments are needed.

At the very least, you need to take an interest in other people. If you find others boring, the fault lies within you for not allowing them to open up and show their interesting sides. There's nothing wrong with loving yourself. But there is something wrong with being so preoccupied with yourself that you poison your social interactions.

Alternately, when you tell stories, don't make it about how funny or awesome *you* are. Make yourself the supporting character, or better yet, tell a story about the person you're talking to through your observations. If you insist on persistently telling a story and speaking, at least take the spotlight off you and make them the hero of those stories.

The more you turn the conversation to the other person and meet that person's need for validation, approval, and acknowledgment, the more they will think you are a great conversationalist. They'll think because you gave them the attention they feel they deserve and you made them feel they matter, *you* are a great person.

Try this: resist the tendency to share something about yourself even if you feel it's extremely relevant. Even if you think it's the most appropriate thing to say, swallow it and let them shine and be the hero of the story. Listen more than you speak. Don't be "that guy" who keeps redirecting the attention back to himself, his needs, and what's important to him. Don't keep redirecting the conversation to that one trip you took or that one job you're excited about. You only want to interject because your ego wants some attention and wants to make itself known.

Try this: next time you talk to somebody, say as little as possible and try to get that person to speak as much as possible. Let them be the sole hero of the conversation, and notice how much they enjoy it. Pretend to yourself they will give you a quiz about the things they've said. Pay attention to what they say and hang on to their every word. Did that feel incredibly unnatural? Then you have some practice to do!

Be Shocked

There are few reactions to what you say that are as gratifying as simple shock. This is when you have surprised the other person in a way that makes them re-evaluate their way of thinking. It brings enormous value for both parties because you feel massively validated and the other party feels informed and educated.

For example, how good would the following sequence feel?

Person: I think the lead in both those movies is actually the same actor.
You: Actually, they're not. It's two different actors, but they've been compared to each other for years and have made jokes about it.
Person: NO WAY! I had no idea! I can't believe it! You have just blown my mind!

Pretty good, right? That shocked and excited reaction will make it feel like a mixture of validation, smugness, superiority, ego, and confidence has just washed over you. It makes you feel as if what you say has a lot of value, and it makes you feel intelligent and validated.

Having someone react with an eyes-wide-open kind of shock is a great feeling. Thus, you should also allow yourself to appear shocked (only occasionally, but far more often than you think you should).

Let's first define what I mean by shock. I don't always mean a slack-jawed look on your face, screaming for the heavens. For most, it's just a bigger reaction than you might have otherwise—an exaggerated reaction. For example, if someone tells you their mother is visiting them that weekend, a normal reaction would be, "That's nice. Family is important." A shocked reaction would be "Wow! That sounds seriously amazing. I hope you have the best time. I'm SO jealous. You must be so excited for that kind of bonding time."

Shock and other exaggerated reactions make people feel invested because you appear invested and you have been *affected*. If you are excited about their mother visiting, then you truly appear to care. You're not just another conversation throughout their day they won't care about or remember later. That's a conversation that people want to be a part of—memorable ones where both parties *care*.

For occasions when an exaggerated reaction simply won't do, that's when real shock comes into play. Pretend that you've just discovered you were adopted as a child. Imagine the facial expressions and "Oh my GODs" you'd be exclaiming. That's the type of shock you should display to others.

If someone mentions something that is **educational or new to you in any way** (in *their* perception), that's the time when a big reaction of shock will do the most good. Pair your body language, voice, mannerisms, and facial expressions with an explicit statement telling them that the information they just shared is exciting and amazing. You can admit your ignorance and how much it surprised you.

You can also tell them you had *no idea* this was true and now you are enlightened. Of course, you need to use your own wording— but you get the formula. A good example is, "Wow, I had no idea. That is seriously huge. I have never thought about it in that way. To be honest, I never even realized that at all."

Why exactly does this work? Massive, massive validation to the secret belief we all have that we are intelligent and influential. You have confirmed their self-perception and that is very satisfying to most people—if not everyone.

Likewise, people also love sharing information in such a way that they look smarter or otherwise more desirable. It encourages people to keep speaking because you have validated them as intelligent or insightful.

They feel compelled to continue showcasing their intelligence and insight.

For many, it's an unexpected treat when we have the opportunity to talk about ourselves or educate someone else about something we know. It feels great when it happens to you. When you flip the script and give others this feeling, rest assured that it feels just as awesome to them.

Many of us walk through our daily lives on autopilot, and shock obliterates that. For those few split seconds, you feel that you've really made a connection and difference to someone. Showing shock is so effective because it bridges a very common gap among people: it takes us from intellectual acceptance to emotional acceptance.

Now to address a question I can feel brewing: is showing shock or other exaggerated reactions manipulative? Isn't it just some form of pandering and faking it?

Absolutely not.

First of all, your goal is to charm and establish a level of comfort. You're not trying to get money out of someone or sell them a product. You're not otherwise trying to get them to do something that's against their interest. You are trying to fill gaps in emotional acceptance and understanding. Acting shocked is just a technique (based on genuine emotion) to build an emotional gateway from person to person. It's no different than getting better at asking small-talk questions.

Second, you already feel the emotions internally. It might be a mild surprise, or a mild reaction of excitement, but you have the emotions inside you already. All you're doing now is bringing them out and exaggerating them so others can feel them. The expression you are sharing comes from a real place inside. It's no different than the singer who realizes they must sing more loudly in a huge theater to make sure everyone can hear them. The melody and lyrics are the same;

the outward expression is all that is changing here.

Mr. Know-It-All and Mr. One-Upper

Once upon a time, there was a boy named Patrick who had a friend named Phil.

They were fairly close friends, but Patrick began to notice a pattern whenever he told a story to their mutual friends in Phil's presence. Phil might listen attentively to Patrick's story, but immediately after, Phil would proclaim something like, "That's cool, but check out what I did last weekend!"

Every single time.

He was the consummate one-upper— someone who has to commandeer the attention and make himself appear better or more exciting than whatever was previously talked about. One-uppers make it a point to use comparison to make themselves feel and appear superior.

A one-upper makes it a point to always turn the focus of the conversation to them. No matter how accomplished you are, no matter what your achievements, they will always find a way to swing the conversation back to them and highlight their own accomplishments. Even if their accomplishments pale in comparison to yours, they will always find an angle that makes them look like a hero. They feel an overwhelming need to be constantly at the center of attention. They're addicted to praise and applause.

Phil was also occasionally a know-it-all—someone who refuses to logically or emotionally validate others so as to position himself as superior. A know-it-all is someone who wants you to know they have knowledge. That's why they act as if what you have to say is old news and that they're really smart. Know-it-alls are driven by insecurity; one-uppers aren't driven as much by insecurity as by their need for approval and praise. These are different drives, but both are annoying attention-seekers who must have the last word.

Know-it-alls and one-uppers are driven by ego, pride, and insecurity. They can't allow themselves to be at peace with other people's levels of accomplishments without feeling threatened themselves.

You need the proper strategies to deal with these types of people because they are easily defensive and volatile—as you might expect when someone's pride and ego are at stake. It might be theirs, but it also might be yours, because one-uppers and know-it-alls tend to bring out the worst in others.

How do you deal with an insecure know-it-all or one-upper?

It's not as easy as just calling them out or making them feel small. Most of the time, that's the last thing you want to do—you might as just insert tension via turkey baster. There are more graceful ways to deal with them.

First, you need to ask yourself whether this occasion is worth getting excited and arguing about. You need to choose your battles carefully. The very nature of a know-it-all or one-upper is that they are protecting their pride and ego. This means they are ready, willing, and eager to make a big deal out of nothing just to protect themselves and display their superiority.

You could create a huge, catastrophic blow-up over something you might not really care about, or which doesn't actually affect you.

Second, don't frame things as a competition. Their egos can't stand being second, so they lock in their sights on being the top dog. That's fine. You don't have to engage them.

Regard them as you might a child who says they are going to be a professional football player when they grow up. "Mhmm, that's nice. Good for you." You essentially concede the space to them. Innocently acknowledge and try to remain on your point after they are done speaking. When you veer away from competition, this takes away their firepower because they realize their ego is safe and there is nothing at stake.

Third, make it look like you're on their side. You can be their biggest cheerleader. Give them the validation they seek for their pride and ego, and then redirect back to your story or accomplishments.

It's likely that once they have been satisfied in that way, they will cede the floor to you. They've gotten what they are after. You are killing them with kindness and giving them what they want.

Fourth, ignore their greatness. This is probably the most infuriating thing you can do to a know-it-all or one-upper. Remember their goal and what they want out of social interactions. So how might they feel when you ignore their claims to greatness?

Ignore and don't engage, because it will compel them to demonstrate their superior intellect. They crave attention, so the best approach is to simply withhold attention from them. If you don't give them the opportunity or acknowledgment, they will eventually learn to stop because they won't get what they are looking for from you.

Let's use an example to illustrate this approach in action. I tell a story about how amazing my travels in Asia were last summer. Phil takes that opportunity to talk about what an amazing time he had at home working at his store and how entertaining it was.

First, is this worth the battle? Depending on your mood, and for the sake of illustration, yes.

Second, can I acknowledge this and move back to my story? Yes, by innocently saying "Oh, that sounds cool, too. What a crazy store! That reminds me of when I was in Thailand ..."

Third, if they persist, you can take a different tack and be their biggest cheerleader:

"Really? Tell me about how you keep track of merchandise. You have the best stories!"

Finally, if they continue to persist, ignoring them is your only choice. After they tell their story, go right on with your story as if they hadn't said a thing. You can also literally just tell them you want to tell them about your travels directly.

When you've got a know-it-all or one-upper, keep in mind that you're dealing with someone potentially fragile. You might say the wrong thing at any minute and cause them to lash out to protect their ego.

You'll notice only a few universal themes in this chapter: defer to others, make it easy for others, and focus on others. Do you see the theme yet?

Chapter 5. The Witty Comeback Machine

As a former fat kid, I used to have a fairly extensive library of witty comebacks for those charming people who liked to point out that I was, indeed, still as fat as I was the day before. Or that they couldn't ride in a car with me for fear of it tipping over. Or that I was so big my Polo brand sport shirt had a *real* horse on it. (This one was pretty clever, I'll admit. Kids really become innovators when they want to insult someone.)

Mind you, I wasn't really that large—just 20 pounds overweight. Luckily for me, it didn't carry over too much into adulthood. It's probably best characterized as extreme "baby fat" fueled by too much candy.

Unlike many of my fat peers, the teasing didn't bother me too much. That's because the bullies mostly stopped picking on me because I developed an arsenal of comebacks whenever I was insulted. These comebacks never failed to either shut people up, or bring them to my side through laughter. It's no wonder that a common origin story for comedians is awkward childhoods where they were bullied, forcing them to defend themselves with their sense of humor. For instance:

You're so fat that horse on your shirt is life-sized!
Comeback: You're wrong. It's WAY bigger. Were you also aware that my Polo sport shirt can be used as a parachute?

Better not ride with Patrick. He's going to tip the car over!
Comeback: You better put six extra wheels on your car for me!

Becoming a witty comeback machine is easier than you think, and it's one of the best conversational tactics you can learn. It doesn't only rear its head when dealing with insults—it is widely applicable once you learn the framework. If it's a bad situation, a witty comeback can diffuse the tension and bring emotional levels back to normal. If it's a good situation, then a witty comeback can make it even jollier.

Whatever the situation, mastering witty comebacks will earn you the respect of other people for your clever wit. It just takes one line—and the shorter and punchier, the better and more effective. A witty comeback does many things simultaneously. It makes people laugh and disarms them while allowing you to appear smart, insightful, and mentally quick.

What did the examples above do? They didn't fight the insult. Rather, they went along with it and even amplified it. They played along and poked fun at themselves as if they were the bully's minion. By taking the insult head-on and rolling with it, they disarmed the bully, who actually wanted a negative reaction instead of assistance. All expectations were defied, and it was even a little bit funny.

That sneaky and subtle way of defending yourself is the definition of a witty comeback. You take a statement and use it as an opportunity to show wit and grace in disarming someone, as opposed to head-to-head conflict. The above examples could easily have been replied to with, "I'm not even that fat. Leave me alone!" or "Well, what about your haircut?" You can imagine how these wouldn't disarm anyone, and indeed would create tension and encourage bullying. In fact, you might make someone want to sock you in the face.

Witty comebacks aren't just for disarming people and easing tension, however. The nature of interaction with friends is that we make fun of each other harder than any bully ever will. Exercising these muscles will make your comebacks better and quicker, instead of having to text them to people 20 minutes after the insult was slung.

We'll get to how to construct a couple of bulletproof witty comebacks, but first, a few words of caution when dealing with this type of fire.

First, generic is bad. You know generic when you hear it, and don't be that person who uses jokes that their grandparent might use. For instance, "I know you are, but what am I?" or "So is your mom."

A witty comeback is judged by how funny or original it is. Using something that is generic or unclever is decidedly neither funny nor creative. Don't just use a generic or template-driven witty comeback that you've seen in a movie or something that better works in a totally unrelated context. And don't use one of the comebacks you thought were hilarious when you were 10. They don't work anymore.

Second, don't act like you can't take a joke.

Of course, witty comebacks need an initial statement to "comeback" to. The vast majority of the time, people are indeed joking when they say something negative about you in your presence. For some people, it's their main way of interacting with friends. It's almost a compliment because they assume you have a sufficient sense of humor and the emotional resiliency to deal with it. Go figure.

Any way you slice it, it's a mode of communication you should have in your bag. The people who *aren't* involved in jokes and good-natured ribbing don't have many friends. If you let it show that you are angry or hurt, it spoils the playful tone you could otherwise enhance with your witty comeback. People think they can joke with you, and you might just prove them 100% incorrect.

For example, if someone made a joke about my fatness, and I got visibly angry, they would likely stop but walk on eggshells around me for days. When someone is uncomfortable with something, they make others uncomfortable as well. If that happens enough times, they'll eventually stop engaging me. Handle the initial negative statement with a wry smirk and with the knowledge that you are about to crush them. Roll with it and dish something back their way.

Third, use the right tone. The best witty comebacks are delivered with 50% indifference. You should never be too excited to thwart someone because that too will show that you are affected by their initial insult.

Indifference is the correct tone because comebacks are about showing that you are cool as a cucumber and whipping out your hidden weapon. If it helps, pretend that you are James Bond delivering a witty retort after a failed murder attempt by a villain. A witty comeback is the verbal equivalent of judo or aikido—using an opponent's words against them. If you take that analogy, you need a certain amount of cool to effectively counteract. Witty comebacks take the power away from the insult hurled.

There are four main types of witty comebacks. None are better than the other, but some might come easier to you more naturally and comfortably.

Type #1: Pick apart their words

Think about the other person's word choice and quickly analyze whether there is another angle or meaning to those words. They say one thing, but is there another interpretation? An easy approach is to interpret their words as overly literal or outlandish. The key is to interpret them in a way that is favorable to you to make it seem as if they complimented you instead of putting you down. It doesn't even have to necessarily be true as long as it sounds plausible enough for them to react to it.

Bob: *You are working as slow as a glacier. Pick it up!*
You: [misinterpreting the word glacier] *You mean I'm super strong and cool under pressure? True.*

Johnny: *This food makes me want to puke.*
You: *Did you know animals sometimes puke when they are extremely excited? So, thank you.*

Type #2: Agree and amplify

The idea here is to agree with whatever the insult was, and then add to it in an absurd way. You amplify the initial sentiment to a degree that is ridiculous. This was my go-to technique to deflect jokes about my weight. If their sentiment is X, then your sentiment should try to be 10X. You are joining in the party against yourself, but also showing security because you are making yourself a bigger butt of the joke.

If you forgot from earlier in this chapter: *You're so fat that horse on your shirt is life-sized!*

Amplification*: Were you also aware that my Polo Sport shirt can be used as a parachute?*

Amplification: *You better put six extra wheels on your car for me!*

Bob: *Your cooking was pretty terrible last time.*
Amplification: *You're lucky you didn't stay until the end of the night. We all got our stomachs pumped. Dinner at my place later tonight?*

Type #3: Reverse and amplify

This is a simple deflection. This is when you get back at them in a subtle way. When someone says you are bad at X, you basically turn it around by saying that they are even worse at X. It's the exact same as the previous type of witty comeback, except instead of directing the amplification at yourself, you direct it to the other person.

Bob: *Your cooking was pretty terrible last time.*
You: *Yeah, but at least I didn't need to get my stomach pumped the way I did after you cooked last time!*

Johnny: *Those shoes are so ugly.*
You: *Yeah, but at least the color of mine don't cause blindness like yours!*

Type #4: Use an outlandish comparison

This brings the conversation into a different sphere and makes both people laugh at the weird outlandish imagery. Go oddball, extreme, and over the top. To use the same framework, you're amplifying (to yourself or the other person) with an analogy here. This doesn't quite throw it back at them; it just deflects and changes the topic out of absurdity and even confusion.

Bob: *Your cooking was pretty terrible last time.*
You: *True, I should have used the eggs as hockey pucks, right?*

Johnny: *Those shoes are so ugly.*
You: *They make you look like Cindy Crawford's beauty mark.*

Witty comebacks are the blood of witty banter, which is being able to take an element of what was said and attack it from a different angle without missing a beat. You should be able to see how this can play out. They are instant retorts that aren't hostile or combative while addressing something gracefully. What more can you ask for?

Word of caution: fight the temptation to rattle them off one after the other. Again, you have to remember that your goal is to get people to like you. You're not trying to prove a point or protect your pride. Too much makes it feel like you are one-dimensional and can't hold a substantive conversation. Firing off one comeback after another can kill whatever level of comfort you've managed to create because you will appear insecure, defensive, and full of bluster.

Roll with the punches a bit more and see the joy in people's eyes as they realize they can engage you in that way.

Self-Deprecation

Some elements of witty comebacks are rooted in self-deprecation, as you may have noticed. Self-deprecation gets a bad rap. When a lot of people think of self-deprecation, they think about Charlie Brown's dejected musings and his glass half-empty way of approaching life. That's not the same; that's just being depressed and trying to get attention for it.

Self-deprecation isn't about throwing yourself a pity party. It's when you can poke fun at yourself and show vulnerability to move a conversation forward. It's tremendously useful because it can simultaneously diffuse tension and show wit—just like snappy comebacks.

Specifically, they make you more human and approachable. Many people have reasons for using self-deprecation, but the types of people who do not use self-deprecation are much more uniform. They are insecure with themselves and uncomfortable exposing their flaws—even in jest. It's too risky for them and it might hit too close to home.

Someone who can use self-deprecation effectively owns up to their flaws and even highlights them. If you don't feel as if you're a good driver, you might be comfortable saying, "I'm such a terrible navigator; every trip we take is the scenic route by accident." If you're comfortable with your weight, you might even be able to say something like, "Yeah, I got pretty out of breath from those five stairs we had to climb."

Your ability to talk about your flaws in such a blasé way makes you appear vulnerable yet secure. All you did was make a joke about how large your flaw is, and it accomplishes many goals simultaneously. Self-deprecation will instantly give others the sense that you are someone who can laugh, be secure, and be joked around with. In professional settings, this might be doubly important, as people are always looking for outlet valves in the workplace.

And if you're in a position above others, or are dealing with a sense of competition or ego, self-deprecating humor works as tension relief. It disarms others and demonstrates that you don't approach them as their superior or competitive—that you're not taking yourself too seriously. It also paves the way for your listeners to consider you as one of them or to view you as a "regular" person.

According to a study on the role of humor in sexual selection conducted by anthropologist Gil Greengross, self-importance and pomposity were found to be the traits most despised in potential sexual mates.

In fact, he found that "Self-deprecating humour can be an especially reliable indicator not only of general intelligence and verbal creativity, but also of moral virtues such as humility."

In other words, humility is far more prized in mates, along with a sense of humor. Being accomplished is attractive; being reluctant to talk about your accomplishments is even more attractive. Who would have thought? Now that you know the big advantages of self-deprecating humor, you also need to understand the inherent dangers.

You can't be like Charlie Brown. You can't do it in such a way that it makes you look like you're compensating for something or truly lacking self-esteem. You don't want to be pathetic.

For example, a statement like, "Oh no, I'm terrible with maps. I'm the worst. Haven't you ever seen me drive? I couldn't get us anywhere. Just give up. Find someone else" sounds as if you're apologizing for your shortcomings and are eaten up by them. It's too much. This doesn't seem like a joke anymore and will make people uncomfortable at your lack of self-esteem.

There's a difference between being humorously self-deprecating and projecting yourself as pathetically inept, and the former is, "I can't do maps, seriously. We'll just end up in Yugoslavia instead of Los Angeles."

Self-deprecating statements often hit close to home, but as long as you are doing it to yourself, you know your boundaries. Make sure the joke is all about you and only you. You don't know everyone's level of confidence or what triggers their insecurities. If you use self-deprecating humor too frequently, it will seem as if you have low self-confidence and self-respect. It will be too many jokes for someone not to notice and take seriously. They won't feel comfortable around you because they'll feel you don't value yourself—so why would they?

Finally, avoid false modesty. People who are actually egomaniacs and full of themselves are often self-aware of appearing so, so they attempt to disguise their conceited nature by engaging in self-deprecating humor. They have a hard time believing in any of their flaws, so their attempts at self-deprecation are forced and often transparent. You can identify these attempts when they are plainly false, or about a tiny flaw that is inconsequential in the grand scheme of things.

To get better at self-deprecation, my first suggestion is to put your Kindle or book down and watch a couple of video clips of Conan O'Brien, the late-night television show host. His delivery might give you some good ideas of the tone we are shooting for. He is a master of delivering a line in a way that is funny and disarming and shows his vulnerability.

It doesn't always have to be spontaneous. You can prepare well ahead of time. The key here is just to make sure the elements are all present.

First, make a list of the things you feel comfortable making fun of yourself about or those things others make fun of you for. These are your negative traits, flaws, idiosyncrasies, unique traits, funny likes and dislikes, funny habits, and so forth. Let's stick with the example of having poor navigational skills.

Decide where your boundaries are.

Second, talk about the flaw you have in direct and unambiguous terms. There are no jokes here; you're merely making a straightforward statement about how you feel. For example, "I have really bad navigational skills. I get lost frequently. Google maps is very important to me." That's pretty clear.

Steps one and two are important for being prepared when the moment comes! It's part of the process you must endure to understand how it works and be prepared for it in the moment spontaneously.

Third, agree and amplify. This is a page from the chapter about witty comebacks—only this time, you can apply it to yourself. Build off the straight statements you collected for step two. Amplify the points they contain to an extreme your flaw might lead to.

For example, "*I get lost very frequently*" is amplified to

- *"I get lost so frequently my phone needs its own phone."*
- *"I get lost so frequently that every trip with me is a hair-raising adventure."*
- *"I get lost on the way to the bathroom at night."*

Another example: you have a pair of shoes that are very old and dirty, but you wear them because they are extremely comfortable. *"My shoes are very old and dirty"* is amplified to:

- *"My shoes are older than the pyramids."*
- *"My shoes are older than your mama."*
- *"These shoes started out white* [even if they are originally black].*"*

Using self-deprecating humor correctly will make you seem clever and socially calibrated. You will be able to disarm people and flow in almost any social setting.

Chapter 6. Conversational Diversity

Even if you use every other tactic in this book to a perfect tee, you might begin to grow bored with the predictable outcomes and increasingly linear structure of your conversations.

You'll say something, you'll get a predictable response, and you'll tell a story that will lead you in a predictable direction. Your conversations might have a good flow, but you might feel bored and flat. You start getting into a routine or groove, and that can be hard to break out of. Suddenly, you're back where you started in having boring conversations that don't engage anyone.

Just as when you get good at anything, things can become stale if they are not challenging. That's why the concept of conversational diversification is important. If you can't learn how to diversify your conversation topics and structures and break out of whatever mode you've grown accustomed to, you are doomed to be limited in your eloquence.

You'd be just like one of my friends from college. Imagine the most pleasant job interview you've ever had. It might have been comfortable, and there might even have been rapport, but in the back of your mind, you knew all along where it was going. That's what interacting with him was like. He had good stories and was interested in what you had to say, but the whole thing just started to feel predictable. There was no depth or spice.

I'd feel as if we were having a great time, but it would simultaneously feel as if we were just going through the motions. It's the "box of the normal conversation." If we talk about a new job, we'd talk about how we liked it and how the coworkers were. I can't quite describe it, but it felt like each topic was a neatly contained compartment to move through. It was more similar to speaking to a stranger in some ways.

We're still good friends, but it can be tough sometimes to say the least. So here are some methods to spice up your conversations and inject some diversity and plain ol' fun into them.

Hypotheticals

A hypothetical is a classic conversational diversification tactic. Okay, that's a fancy term for what really amounts to, "Hey, what would you do if …" and "What do you think about …"

But here's what happens when you throw a hypothetical into your conversation. You inject exponentially the amount of variability and unpredictability possible because it's likely something your conversation partner has never considered, and the hypothetical you pose will be something that has no clear or correct answer. Instead, something hopefully exciting comes out of it and you get to discuss something that would never have come up otherwise.

Use hypotheticals to see how people react and how their minds work. You'll learn something about them from how they answer, and you can treat the hypothetical itself like an inkblot test—how they answer probably says something about them. In the end, wherever it goes will probably be more interesting than an interview!

The easiest way to make a conversation awkward or to introduce dead space is to ask questions that can easily be answered by a simple yes or no. Open-ended questions allow for creativity. They allow people to dig into their memory banks, come up with random associations, or otherwise trigger their imagination. With that said, your hypothetical question should be challenging enough so that the recipient actually needs to be a bit creative in answering the question.

The secret to hypotheticals is to make them appear spontaneous. Ask for their opinion on something out of curiosity. You don't want to come off as contrived or like you're reading from a script. That's going to make you look ingenuous. And you don't want to seem as if you have some sort of agenda.

Adding a one- to two-sentence backstory as to why this thought "spontaneously" popped into your mind tends to help.

Finally, keep in mind that when you use these, you must also have an answer prepared for the hypothetical you ask. You can step in with your answer while they are formulating theirs—and you should have thought about this answer beforehand so you can be prepared and rehearse it. Don't be in a situation where you don't know the answer to your own hypothetical. You don't need a definitive answer, but you at least need a stance or opinion. There's nothing worse than your conversation partner saying, "I don't know" and you also saying, "I don't know." Nothing else will fill that space besides awkward silence.

Here are some examples of hypothetical questions you can toss into your conversations like a grenade. It's a good rule of thumb to have a few prepared and up your sleeve for when you sense you are falling into some type of routine or pattern.

Type #1: What would you do if …

Example: What would you do if the waiter from lunch screamed at you to give him a bigger tip?

Type #2: Would you rather have this or that?

Example: Would you rather be four inches shorter or 16 inches taller?

Type #3: My friend just did/said this … What would you have done?

Example: My friend just called out his boss for working too much. Can you imagine that? What would you have done?

Type #4: What if you were in this situation ...

Example: What if your coworker was stealing your food from the fridge every day? How would you handle that?

Type #5: Which of the following ...

Example: Which do you think is better: super cold winters or hot summers?

Type #6: Who do you think ...

Example: Which of us do you think got the best grades in school? Or the worst?

Think Out Loud

This is a rather simplistic way of phrasing it, but thinking out loud can introduce quite a bit of conversational diversity. We filter ourselves far too much, and while it's called for sometimes, it doesn't always help.

If we just voice our inner monologue about what we're thinking about during our day, this can be quite an icebreaker. Share your thoughts about your surroundings or what you observe around you. Share what you are doing, what you are seeing, what you are thinking, and what you are wondering. Thinking out loud can also just be voicing your feelings, such as "I'm so happy with the sunshine right now" or "I can't believe the coffee here is so expensive!"

This will lead to a more open flow of communication. Others will feel less guarded around you and that can lead to a higher level a mutual comfort. It's also bound to be more interesting than filling the silence with a question that no one cares about.

Just say what's on your mind and you are inviting others to speak, but it's not a demand.

The added benefit is you'll probably end up being that person who says what everyone is thinking but is afraid to say. Maybe they're just shy or want to seem polite. Whatever it is, they are thinking it, but they feel it's not proper to voice their thoughts aloud. If you become that person who is the first to say what everyone is thinking, you break the ice.

People will feel they can trust you and be comfortable around you because you actually have the guts to say what they wanted to say. At least you'll bring up some common ground that others can comment on.

Analogies

An analogy paints a mental picture for someone so they can understand you better. It snaps people out of autopilot and makes them engage and react.

Of course, they are also good for making what you say memorable and easy to grasp. You could be talking about something completely abstract, and connect by using a simple analogy.

Personally, I know nothing about cars. But if someone were to describe a car's capabilities to me in terms of gym exercises and routines, I would instantly comprehend.

When do you use an analogy? When you are trying to explain something or make someone understand your meaning. It also serves to bring flavor to an otherwise bland line of discussion.

Analogies need to be relatable, so you need to choose analogies that the vast majority of people will instantly understand. After all, there's nothing worse than having to explain the analogy intended to explain a concept. So the broader your analogy types, the higher the likelihood people will connect to it. It can also involve an experience or concept that people can connect with.

Take sports, for example. Most people know the basic rules of baseball, so keeping that in your pocket can be valuable. Now, what are the main and recognizable aspects of baseball?

Baseball:
- is boring to some
- allows players to stand idly for hours
- is played on a large green field
- involves sticks and balls
- periodic running

If you're having a boring conversation about dogs, for instance: *"The way that dog is running from spot to spot reminds me of a baseball player running the bases."* You didn't do anything particularly special except compare the current topic to something completely different.

For another example, take food. Eating works because everybody eats, and there are some foods that everybody eats.

Pasta is:
- long and thin

- soft when wet
- hard when dry
- tan in color
- deliciously unhealthy
- associated with Italian food, mostly

"The way that dog is lying down makes me think of overcooked pasta."

Here are a couple more for you:

"This reminds me of Walmart because it's so big and impersonal."

"He has the body of melted ice cream."

Third-Party References

The final way to create some conversational diversity is to use third-party references—another fancy name for a simple concept.

"My friend told me …" or "I was just reading about …"

These utilize other people as reference points to introduce new topics and interesting topical matters that might be completely unrelated. This is when you're ditching the current line of conversation and sparking it with something engaging of your choice.

When you use these phrases, you naturally segue into something entirely new. You prevent the conversation from getting stale by intentionally derailing it. You can also look at this as simply changing the topic, but in an intentional manner. These phrases are important because they make your inquiries seem natural and organic, as opposed to playing a game of trivia or "Did you know?"

And again, while these should always come off as spontaneous, you can prepare for these interesting subjects far ahead of time. You want to create third-party references that are compelling or at least open up room for debate. Why bother switching topics if you're just going to switch to a dud? For this reason, interpersonal matters are often good to use.

Just as with hypotheticals, you need to have at least a stance or opinion on the matter in case they reflect it back to you. Finally, make sure to ask for their opinion directly so they know it's a prompt they should respond to.

"**I read an article recently** about men feeling just as insecure as women at the beach. What do you think about that?"

"**A friend recently told me that** his mother interferes with his girlfriend's schedule a lot. What do you think about that?"

Using these phrases allows you to bring up anything you want. Nothing will seem too random because you properly grounded it in the right context. The person you are talking to feels more engaged because you are asking for their opinion. And you've just created some entertainment and friendly debate for yourself. Just like with hypotheticals, you never know how they are going to react, so it's fun to see how unpredictable things can quickly become.

No matter how good you are at conversing, sometimes it can feel like you're stuck in a box. Sure, it might be a box of your own choosing, but it gets stale all the same. There are many ways you can inject some diversity into your conversation so you yourself get surprised with the outcome.

Chapter 7. Conversational Diversity Part 2

You didn't think I'd stop with just those methods for conversational diversity in the previous chapter, did you? There are endless possibilities, so I want to introduce a few more small ways you can snap people out of their zombie conversations and make them engage and pay attention. As mentioned, it doesn't matter how good you are at conversations—you'll eventually work yourself into comfortable routines and patterns. These inevitably grow boring, so injecting some novelty can be beneficial for everyone involved.

Personal Compliments

A compliment can go a long way, but you already knew that. Any run-of-the-mill compliment won't do much to improve the level of your conversation.

But a compliment about something uniquely personal is something that people cannot resist and that will open them up immensely.

This typically takes three forms: something new, something they are likely self-conscious about, and something that is uniquely personal to them or idiosyncratic (like a habit or behavior). The common thread is that these tend to be aspects that people have put conscious thought into. In other words, they have made intentional decisions to present themselves in these ways, so when you compliment them on a new jacket, you aren't just complimenting the jacket; you're complimenting their fashion sensibilities, taste, and overall presentation.

Those may not sound easy to parse, but this requires only a slightly more intense level of observation on your part. For example, particularly bright clothing or "statement" pieces such as blue suede shoes—those are definitely things people do to stand out and are simultaneously self-conscious about. They have made a conscious choice and are thinking, "I hope people notice and like these as much as I do!" Complimenting these pieces will validate them and make them happy that other people are noticing them without them having to wave their arms and point to their shoes, screaming, "Look how *BLUE* they are!"

That's what compliments about personal elements do—they make people feel that others see them as the unique snowflakes they see themselves as. It's a great feeling, isn't it?

This is a good rule of thumb for compliments, but is it conversational diversity? Surprisingly, yes.

There are many things that are impersonal about people, like common or generic traits. These are low-hanging fruits that people usually compliment on. Complimenting someone's eyes or smile is nice and all, but probably something they've heard countless times before. It wasn't their choice, so it really amounts to, "Congratulations on the good face."

I'm willing to bet most people, especially people with good faces, would prefer to be complimented on their opinions, thought processes, or idiosyncrasies. Even a new haircut or even a new car; people are bound to be self-conscious about those things and concerned about how they will be received. Pay homage and they will feel gratified.

The more personalized and more particular, the stronger the person is impacted.

In the movie *When Harry Met Sally*, there is a motif of Sally ordering meals in restaurants in an extremely particular and picky way. She requires many substitutions and modifications in a way that probably enrages every waiter she comes across. It is something only she would do, and yet, it's something that would likely be a monumental compliment because it is so uniquely personal.

You're commenting on the outward manifestation of their personality, and that's validation of the highest kind. At least, don't fall prey to paying compliments that they've probably heard earlier in the week.

Be Unpredictable

Another approach to conversational diversity is to give interesting answers to common questions. In other words, become a little bit unpredictable in how you engage others.

Predictable conversation is bad conversation. It's boring and leads you mentally check out of a conversation. For instance, *how are you (good), how was your weekend (great), how is your wife (she's awesome)?*

I'm bored already. Those are common answers to common questions. So start by giving an unexpected answer to a common question that people normally give milquetoast answers to or altogether overlook. You will catch people off guard in the best way and they'll be a combination of shocked and delighted. Remember from earlier in the book that you should avoid strictly exchanging information types of conversations? This is another instance of how it can sneak back in without you realizing it.

For example, how do you deal with the question, "What do you do?" and "Where are you from?" There are a few ways.

Most people will probably give a one-word answer, or at best, a generic one-phrase answer. At worst, you will receive an ambiguous and confusing answer that you won't know how to reply to.

So instead of saying, "I'm an engineer" and "I'm from Kentucky," you can easily give a more interesting answer. After all, people don't really care about the literal answers to these questions. They just want to hear something interesting they can engage with you about—if the answer is interesting *and* gives substantive information, that's just a bonus. Unless they also happen to be an engineer from Kentucky, it's unlikely that those answers will be very compelling.

The first way to answer mundane questions is to dance around the real answer. You are giving information, but in almost riddle-form.

"I type things in the computer for a living and I'm from a state no one knows anything about except the Kentucky Derby."

You put an otherwise mundane answer into an interesting form that requires some thought and almost decoding. While the facts are exactly the same, your presentation makes you look more insightful and like you don't take yourself seriously. It simply gives people something to respond to or ask about in the case they aren't an engineer or from Kentucky.

Another example: when somebody asks you what you're doing in a café, you can either say, "I'm working" or "I'm leeching off the café's Wi-Fi for a while." The latter emphasizes your ability to spot logical connections and highlights your humor.

The second way to be unpredictable is to literally make something up. If everyone expects a "normal" answer or at least one that fits their narrative of you, this will ensure that people are thrown off by what you say. You can say the opposite of what they expect, or just go over the edge and shoot for something absurd or outlandish. The key is to deliver it as if it is completely normal for you.

"What do you do?"
"I actually work for the FBI and can't really talk about it. It does involve Africa and Russia, though."

If you really want to have a bit more fun with it, you can answer common questions with stories such as the above, and then stay in character for a bit to try to rationalize the story and create an entire backstory while thinking out loud.

Some other common questions that can be answered in a creative way include:

- "Where did you go to school?"
- "Do you have any siblings?"
- "What did you study?"
- "How was your weekend?"
- "How long have you been living here?"

Warning: if you make it a point to always answer questions in weird or unusual ways, it can get annoying very quickly. Don't get stuck with just one strategy. If you overdo this, it will make you seem as if you can't answer a question honestly or really be engaged. Or worse, it will appear that you are trying to avoid any serious discourse. If you become predictably unpredictable, you become obnoxious.

This particular way of spicing up a conversation works best for close-ended questions. These are the questions that have a fixed range of answers. You're just coming up with a creative way to phrase an otherwise straightforward answer.

Sarcasm? No Way

Sarcasm is a way for people to say things without saying them. Think about how Chandler Bing from the television show *Friends* talks. If he says something is wonderful, he says *it's wonnnnderful* in a tone that immediately lets you know that he thinks the opposite.

Sarcasm functions like a social cue—both are ways to express something without having to explicitly say it. In that way, it's a great device for handling uncomfortable topics or pointing out the elephant in the room without directly offending people (or pointing). It allows us to walk a tightrope, as long as we don't fall into the pit of passive-aggressiveness.

At some level, most of us can appreciate sarcasm because we know what is being accomplished. It can even be the basis for your own personal brand of humor. Standup comics often use it to great effect.

Chances are, you are already using it regularly without being fully aware of it. Sarcasm is mostly used as friendly banter with a friend or acquaintance with whom you are comfortable saying something negative. Sarcasm is usually used to poke fun at someone or something, and is heavily context- and audience-dependent. In some social circles, appropriate levels of sarcasm are not only welcomed, but required.

If your annoying coworker understood sarcasm better, they might be as funny as they think they are. For the most part, sarcasm is saying the *opposite* of (1) an objective fact, (2) a subjective emotion, or (3) a thought. It makes a contradictory statement about a situation to either emphasize or downplay its effect.

Objective fact: Bob plays Tetris at work constantly.

Sarcastic statement: *Bob, you are the busiest man I know.*

Subjective emotion or thought: It is hilarious that Bob plays Tetris at work constantly.

Sarcastic statement: *Bob deserves a medal for worker of the year.*

Here's another one.

Objective fact: There is a surprising amount of traffic lately.

Sarcastic statement: *What are we going to do when we get to our destination super early?*

Subjective emotion or thought: I hate traffic so much.

Sarcastic statement: *This traffic is the best part of my day.*

That's the first and most common use of sarcasm. Let's lay out a framework for different types of sarcasm and exactly when and how you can use it. You'll be surprised how formulaic and methodical you can get with this, and subsequently with humor.

When someone says something or does something very obvious, you respond by saying something equally obvious.

Bob: "That road is very long."
You: "You are very observant."

Bob: "It's so hot today!"
You: "I see you're a meteorologist in training."

Poor Bob: "This menu is huge!"
You: "Glad to see you've learned to read!"

Another application of sarcasm is when something bad happens. You say something about how that good or bad event reflects on the other person.

If it's good, you say that it reflects badly on them; if it's bad, you say it reflects well on them.

Bob: "I dropped my coffee mug."

You: "You've always been so graceful."

Bob: "I got an F on my math test."
You: "Now I know who to call when my calculator breaks."

You observe Poor Bob dropping a cup of coffee and state, "You would make a great baseball catcher. Great hands!"

Proper delivery is crucial for sarcasm. This can mean the difference between people laughing at your sarcastic joke, or thinking that you're serious in your sentiment and a jerk. You have to make it clear that you're being sarcastic and give them a sign indicating so. Otherwise, people will feel uncomfortable at the uncertainty. Are you just being mean, or are you trying to be funny?

The most common way to do this is with a combination of a deadpan vocal tone and a wry smile or smirk. With deadpan delivery, you don't laugh while you're saying it; you appear completely serious. Then you break into a smile to alleviate the tension and clue them into your true intention.

Now that you know when to deliver sarcastic remarks, it's also important to learn about how to receive them and be a good audience. Let's pretend that you are Poor Bob from earlier, and insert a reply for him.

Bob: "That road is very long"
You: "You are very observant."
Bob: "You know it. I'm like an eagle."

Bob: "It's so hot today!"
You: "I see you're a meteorologist in training."
Bob: "I can feel it in my bones. It's my destiny."

Poor Bob: "This menu is huge!"
You: "Glad to see you've learned to read!"
Redeemed Bob: "I can also count to ten."

You need to amplify their statement and what they are implying. Does this look familiar? It's a self-deprecating remark + a witty comeback!

When you respond to sarcasm this way, it creates a greater bond. Everybody is comfortable, and you create a funny situation and potential for greater banter. And just as important, you don't come off as a bad sport or someone who can't take a joke.

A lot of people who rely on sarcastic humor, pretty much on an automatic basis, are actually masking passive-aggressive personalities. They're constantly using sarcasm as a defense mechanism to hide their true feelings. They use sarcasm to pass off their otherwise negative emotions. They might be doing this to you, so it's important to know how to sidestep their subconsciously vicious attacks.

In the end, it's your choice as to how you want your interactions to go. You can control them, but you'll have to deviate from your established routines.

Chapter 8. Can You Stop That?

Sometimes, just as you might fear, you are indeed the cause for awkward silences. As covered, awkward moments occur when we don't have a clear sense of how to move forward. We don't want to misinterpret people or say something that takes away from the moment—so we say nothing and subsequently our minds go blank.

We tend to have moments such as asking a chubby coworker when the baby is due if we're not aware of the potential consequences of our actions and words. So what are some obvious and less obvious causes of these moments you wish you could take back? What should you *stop* more and do less?

Laughter That Isn't Infectious

We all have fake laughs. No matter how honest we think we are, or how much we hate sugarcoating things to people, we still utilize our fake laughs on a daily basis.

Here's the thing about most of us—we're inherently nice! We want people to like us, we want social situations to go smoothly, and we want awkward silences to die. Most importantly, we don't want people to feel bad about themselves when they inevitably make a bad joke. So we throw them a pity chuckle.

Fake laughter is the lubricant that salvages many conversations. It fills empty space and gives you something to do when you have no idea what to say. It keeps conversation rolling and gives the appearance of engagement even if you're bored out of your mind. Appearances, as it turns out, do matter sometimes. If you're speaking with the head honcho of your company, you know that your best fake laughter will be put to the test because you want them to like you.

And sometimes we depend on the fake laughter of other people to prevent us from feeling self-conscious or stupid.

So we laugh at people's jokes. Laughter is pretty much an integral part of our daily lexicon—but that doesn't mean we like it, and the more we have to do it with someone, the more tiring—and ultimately unpleasant—it is to talk to them.

Obviously, fake laughter from others is something we want to avoid, so what is the biggest step we can take to prevent it?

Never laugh at your own jokes, at least not first.

The biggest culprit for people to use their fake laughter and ultimately get tired of talking to you is when you laugh at your own joke loudly and proudly, and without looking to the other person for a reaction … especially when the jokes aren't great, time after time. Think about it.

Monica makes a mediocre joke and laughs at it. Don't you feel like you have to give her a fake chuckle to keep the conversation moving and give her the reaction she is seeking?

Okay, so you force a smile onto your face and expel some breath from your lungs. No big deal. Then Monica does it again. And again. And again. And your facial muscles start to hurt because of how much you have to contort it into a fake, glazed-over smile. I'm annoyed just writing about it and I don't even know Monica. In person, I'm sure I would grow tired in record time and make an excuse to wander away from Monica.

That's what laughing at your own jokes first, without gauging how the other person receives it, will do to your conversation partners. When you always laugh first, you're *imposing your will* on the conversation partner and essentially telling them how to feel.

That's like talking about politics and then subtly telling them how you want them to vote. The worst part is that you aren't able to hear their opinions, so the conversation slowly becomes a platform for you to showcase your alleged humor ... and that is not a conversation most people enjoy being a part of.

It's a very slippery slope to becoming "that guy" or "that girl" that people try to avoid at parties because they don't notice that a person wants to talk about something else besides their jokes.

There's also an element of the inability to read social cues if you're always laughing first, loudly and proudly. Social cues are the little signs and hints people give off that say what they're really thinking. For example, a common social cue is that when someone leans back with their arms crossed and looks around the room behind you, they aren't interested in what you have to say. What cues can you observe if you're reacting first and forcing them to abandon their social cues to match you? You could be throwing your head back in laughter while the other person is slowly inching away and you might not even notice.

Another element to always laughing first at your own jokes is it leaves you completely unable to gauge how funny you actually are. Without any proper and uninfluenced reactions, you are living in a world where you only hear laughter—laughter of your own that you manufacture. This can lead to an inflated sense of self—I'm sure you have friends that think they are hilarious because all they do is hear their own laughter.

Others might laugh with you, but it doesn't mean they think you're funny. Always laughing first is usually a reaction born out of insecurity and the fear of conversational rejection, which is essentially silence after a joke. You start by wanting to *seed* laughter and make sure that you get the response you are looking for, and after a while, it becomes a subconscious habit you can't break out of.

Not getting the emotional reaction that you want can be embarrassing or downright paralyzing to some people, so it makes sense that they want to seed the emotion, in a sense. It's understandable and we've all felt it when we were feeling shy or nervous about something—nervous laughter, anyone?

But remember the burden and feeling you are creating in others when you laugh first, at yourself, without gauging the response in others. After all, it's hard to listen and observe when your mouth is making noise. The realization that you may be hamstringing conversation with this simple no-no can be transformational.

"Creepiness"

And before you say that this is just a male problem, it's not. This can apply equally to males and females. It just happens to manifest more in females because, well, you'll see.

You've heard people call others creepy before behind their backs. People may even say the same about you behind your back. Obviously, it's something you want to avoid that can cause far worse than awkward silence. But what does it really mean and how can you avoid it?

It turns out scientists have actually attempted to quantify "creepiness." The first theory comes to us from evolutionary psychologists, who tend to view much of our behavior through the lens that it helped us survive when we were still living in fear of wild animal attacks every day. More specifically, the feeling of dread or discomfort from creepy people is referred to as *agency detection*, which means you become aroused and alert if you sense danger. Of course, this is known as the *fight-or-flight instinct*, which is the choices our body prepares itself for when danger is perceived.

So that's why the feeling of creepiness exists; what exactly is it looking for? If you are feeling negative from a gun pointed at you, that's not creepiness. If you are about to jump off of a bridge, that's not creepiness either. It can make your hairs stand up, give you goosebumps, and send chills down your spine. But it's still different. It isn't just emotional or physical harm that we want to steer clear of, even though those create feelings of danger and discomfort as well. No, creepiness is something that takes a very specific combination of factors to arouse.

A study from Knox College led by Francis McAndrew can lend some knowledge to this area. The researchers gave over 1300 participants a questionnaire on the traits and actions that would make them label someone "creepy." The questionnaire allowed the participants to rate sample behaviors, occupations, and even hobbies on a creepiness scale. The participants were both male and female (1029 females and 312 males), and they were able to generate five major actions that made someone get called the C word.

1. Appear to be watching and staring at someone before interacting with them.
2. Touching someone an inappropriate amount.
3. Frequently steering the conversation to sex.
4. Asking to take a picture of people alone.
5. Asking for personal details about someone's family.

Other actions that didn't make the top five include standing too close to someone and violating their personal space, and avoiding all eye contact. Other findings include the fact that clowns, taxidermists, and funeral directors were seen as creepy occupations, and creepy hobbies included collecting dolls or insects, and watching people (such as voyeurism).

Taking a step back, it's clear that all of these actions do indeed invoke the word creepiness. We make an uncomfortable face and cringe when we imagine someone doing it to us. The worst part is the perpetrators likely have no idea of the impression they are creating.

One of the common threads of all of the actions is that there is a sense of ambiguity and uncertainty. People weren't sure if they were truly in danger or should be alert— sometimes that's worse, isn't it? When you know you have a big speech in front of 1000 people, you can prepare yourself for it. But when there is an ambiguous threat, you don't know if it's coming or what form it might be in. Uncertainty about a threat evokes far worse fear. Unpredictability, while in other parts of this book can serve to invigorate you, compounds on dread and fear in the face of a potential threat. It also paralyzes us and leaves us unable to respond or act because we simply don't know what we should do.

There are countless other ways you can try to define or quantify creepiness, but deciphering the meaning of the word isn't the important part; understanding seven actions you should avoid is the important part.

Shut Up

Sometimes, if we're not causing awkward silence, we're just causing conflict with our big, fat mouths. Case in point: advice and when it's unsolicited.

How many times have you heard somebody excuse rude and hurtful comments by claiming that they are simply calling it how they see it, or being brutally honest? Chances are you've come across a few people who communicate this way, and it's also probable that they weren't the most likable people you've ever encountered.

Brutal honesty most often means criticizing others without any tact or sense of compassion. Supposedly, those blunt comments and criticisms are meant to be beneficial to whomever they are directed at, and they are only hurtful if taken personally or defensively.

The thing about brutal honesty, though, is that nobody actually prefers it, and in most cases, it just comes across as deliberately mean. The vast majority of the time, negativity just isn't necessary because it's possible to accomplish your goal by providing feedback or criticism in a mature and considerate way. Complaining and nitpicking about things that aren't important just makes you come across as judgmental and abrasive—making others feel small so that you can feel big.

Honesty itself is very useful, and having the tact to be honest in a way that doesn't put people down is an invaluable life skill to have. But far too many people think that honesty is socially acceptable in any form. The simple truth of the matter is that if you want to always say how you feel without any kind of a filter, people just won't like you. Unless, of course, you are the first brutally honest person ever to think and feel positive things all the time.

There's a particular type of brutal honesty, tough love, that's commonly used by parents to teach their young children important lessons. But tough love is not for everyone or every situation, and is probably even counterproductive for raising children in a lot of scenarios, as the lesson they learn may come with an unhealthy hit to their self-esteem.

Any time that you feel the need to criticize somebody, ask if that criticism can actually help them. If not, keep it to yourself. If so, frame it in a tactful way that doesn't come off as a personal attack.

For example, say you've got a friend who dresses really poorly and it adversely affects their attractiveness to others. If that's something your friend cares about and would want to know, then a productive way to help your friend is to suggest something that you think would look good on them, and then compliment them when they do dress well in order to give positive reinforcement. Except in serious cases, positive reinforcement can

work a whole lot better than criticism—
especially criticism that's framed as honesty,
but lacking any practical advice.

But now let's imagine that your friend has
never given any indication that they want to
improve their attractiveness or that they care
about their wardrobe. Now anything you say
in the form of advice is unsolicited, which just
makes you annoying.

As a general rule, giving unsolicited advice
isn't going to be received well, no matter how
good your intentions are. When people vent
or rant to you about some problems in their
lives, the socially intelligent response is to let
them fulfill their purpose for speaking without
interrupting them to interject your own
solution. Talking about problems serves as
emotional catharsis—meaning that it's often
a solution all of its own, and you can be a part
of that solution just by listening.

Finally, one of the most socially
counterproductive things you can do is to
make pedantic corrections of people.

Anything that indirectly implies that you are above others will make you less likeable, plain and simple. You may think that people want or should want to be corrected when they error, but when those errors are unimportant and don't hurt anybody, it's not your responsibility or social prerogative to point them out.

So do yourself and everybody else a favor— shut up and stop interjecting your opinions and advice when nobody asks or cares to hear them.

The common theme from each of these social mistakes that people make is that they can be avoided just by shutting up more often. You may only exhibit one or two of these behaviors personally, or even none of them if you are already highly skilled socially. It's also possible that, through introspection, you could realize you are guilty of almost all of them from time to time.

It's good to analyze when you've made these mistakes in the past, as it can show the areas that you should personally focus on building more awareness in the future. That being said, there's no use in beating yourself up over those mistakes, because we all do these things to some degree. Not knowing when to shut up doesn't automatically make you unlikable; it simply inhibits you from reaching your full social potential.

If you build your awareness about when it's appropriate to talk and when it's better to listen or be silent, you'll improve the depth of your relationships and be more enjoyable company for the people in your life. In the famous words of the 19th century actor Will Rogers, "Never miss a good chance to shut up."

For the purposes of this chapter, his words might be better changed to, "Never miss a good chance to stop doing that!" Sometimes avoiding the negative is just as important as doing something positive; avoiding all negatives will arguably do more for you. If you loved someone but their body odor stank so badly it made your eyes water whenever you were around them, would you be able to persist? At worst, avoiding social negatives will make you more easy to accept—not the worst thing in the world.

Chapter 9. Keep It Flowing

The concept of flow in a conversation is pretty much the antithesis of an awkward silence. Flow is when you feel comfortable and no pressure to say something. When there's no pressure, a silence simply becomes a silence, not an awkward, pregnant pause.

You can view the following as tactics specifically to achieve flow and keep a back-and-forth going, or just as methods to engage people better so they'll always have something to say or respond to.

Engage on Mutual Interests

The essence of a great conversation is a two-way exchange. Both parties are invested, care, and show interest in the other person. Ideally, this happens even if one party is not inherently interested in a topic.

If this isn't happening, then what exactly is going on in the conversation? It's a topic that only one person cares about, or it's a topic that neither person cares about. The former is frustrating and boring for the other person, and the latter is boring for both and commonly known as small talk.

It sounds so simple, but at the very least you can find a topic of mutual interest. You can't just talk about things that only you are interested in. Others might be polite and put up with you for a bit, but eventually they will leave at the first chance they get.

Whenever you switch to a new topic, especially one that you are interested in, you must gauge other people's reactions. Look into their eyes, at their smiles (fake or not),

and at their tone of voice to ascertain their
level of engagement.

Most people won't tell you straight out with
actual words that they couldn't care less
about a topic, so you have to look at their
actions. Words can lie and be polite for
courtesy's sake, but actions can't.

Insist Others Go First

When you start speaking simultaneously with
someone, fighting for airspace, always insist
on letting them go first by saying, "Oh, what
were you saying?" This happens more
frequently than we realize, but most of the
time we just ignore other people and
steamroll ahead with our own statements.

You'll both start speaking simultaneously, and
one of two things will happen.

First, the other person may drop out to cede
the floor to you. That's courteous of them.
After you finish your thought, immediately
ask them what they were going to say, and if

it was what you just mentioned. They may not always do this, though; you can't control it. They might also be doing it out of courtesy and not truly listen to you.

Second, and this is my recommendation, cede the floor to them. Insist that they speak first.

This you can control. Take control of the interruption scenario. Let them finish their thoughts. Insist that they go first, and when you respond, try not to simply repeat the point you were going to make. Try to actually acknowledge and then respond to their words, even if that means completely ditching the point you wanted to make. If you insist on making the same point, at least change the beginning of your sentence to acknowledge them. For instance, "Yes, I do see your point. I don't think of it that way. That makes a lot of sense. But what I was saying was …"

You're still going to speak your mind, but factoring in direct acknowledgment will immediately make others feel heard and ease their tension. It shows respect and that their input actually made it into your head.

This is crucial because bad conversationalists talk to people as if they're just giving a speech, as if there is one designated speaker and listener. It makes it seem as if you have a canned speech, and regardless of what the other person says, you just hit a pause button while they spoke, then hit the play button and continued talking the minute they stopped talking.

Converse

As opposed to debating, persuade or subtly argue. This tactic can be tricky because many people want to feel like they are winning in whatever they do. Even when they are engaging with friends, they might feel like their egos are at stake.

Keep in mind your primary goal should be quite simple—to engage and build rapport. You're not finding avenues to stroke your ego. You are not looking to demonstrate your intellectual superiority by crushing somebody verbally. You shouldn't be hunting for that elusive moment where you can say, "I knew it" or "I told you so!"

The secret to avoiding or fighting against this tendency is to consciously change your focus. Don't focus on being right; that sours your conversation. Your focus should be on simply being comfortable and enjoying the company of the other person in a nonjudgmental manner. If you have a difference in opinion, seek to discover why and not change it. When's the last time you actually changed someone's long-held stance as a result of a casual conversation, anyway? Probably never.

This is especially true when it comes to matters of taste and opinion—for instance, if someone were to proclaim their favorite fruit is mango, and you set out to prove that pineapples are superior. Are you really going to convince someone that their subjective taste is wrong, that their *taste buds* are wrong? It's unlikely, and by harping on this, you begin to alienate people and appear overbearing and bossy.

Whatever you are disagreeing about probably makes no impact on your life. If you feel like you're debating or even trying to persuade, stop! You have to catch yourself when it comes to the natural tendency to debate. Again, this doesn't come easy because our natural tendency is to feel defensive and push back. To present your opinion in a way that doesn't lead to debates, just express it and then *stop*. It really is that simple. Simply express your opinion and leave it at that. You don't need beat people over the head with it; if they care enough, they will ask.

The underlying issue here is that you are not being open-minded or accepting of others' views. While that's an issue for someone else's book, at least become aware of your tendencies. Don't fall into the slippery slope of feeling that you have to prove the other person wrong. Agreeing to disagree is a simple saying but hard to achieve in reality because of the burning feeling when someone's opinion is different from yours. But do yourself a favor and at least keep it to yourself.

Don't be the person that always seems to have a point to prove, because that person quickly becomes avoided at all social gatherings.

Acknowledge Everything

One time my friend John was hiking, and it seemed as if his companion, Lily, wasn't listening to him at all, or even acknowledging anything he was saying.

He was trying to ask deep questions about her emotions and motivations, and all he got was an occasional "Uh huh" or "I guess." The rest of the time it was pure silence and John felt as if he was talking to a wall or to himself. He was frustrated and was starting to feel intentionally disrespected.

John felt the tension growing with every step up the mountain, and dramatically, at the mountain's peak, he asked if he had angered her. No, she was just massively dehydrated and could barely put one foot in front of the other let alone speak.

Now, obviously this is not an everyday happening, but the emotions and feelings involved are fairly common. To some degree, this is what happens every day when you fail to acknowledge what people say, either big or small.

To be a great conversationalist, you have to be *in* the conversation. This doesn't just mean speaking. It means listening, listening some more, and then paying attention to what the other person says and acknowledging everything. Make them feel that they matter even if you aren't listening or caring.

Great conversations are always two-way streets, and two-way streets work best when both sides feel as if they matter.

Anything people say or do, even with their face or body language, matters to some degree, whether they're doing it consciously or subconsciously. They're doing it for a response. It makes them feel validated and accepted when you acknowledge that they are communicating with you. This is why it's so important to acknowledge everything the other person sends you, even if you simply acknowledge it with a simple "Hm" or little grunt.

This isn't a small, common sense point that you can just assume is occurring. You might think you are doing this, but you probably aren't.

Imagine that you make 10 statements, and all 10 aren't acknowledged. Now imagine that you make 10 statements, and all 10 are acknowledged at least with "interesting point" or an agreeing chuckle.

The cumulative effect is startling. Even when people insist they are just thinking out loud or talking to themselves, most of the time they are really looking for feedback—not silence. Aside from acknowledging everything verbal, you should also be on the lookout for nonverbal body language and facial expressions you should acknowledge and react to.

If you were to, for example, notice someone's eyebrows shoot up when you say something about Iceland, that's as good as their verbally saying, "Really?!" Pay attention to these nonverbal signals and acknowledge them. Ask if they have something to add or what about your statement surprised them. Ask them what they were going to say. Don't just let them go through several facial expressions and verbal ticks or strange sounds while you keep unloading what you have to say.

Of course, you have to do this in a way that's not confrontational. Instead, ask in a way that pushes the conversation forward. The best approach is to ask in a curious way. Let the other person know that you're genuinely interested in why they raised their eyebrows or why their eyes popped when you said something.

The reason so many people fail to acknowledge the other person is that they are selfish. They want to finish their own thoughts, and they prioritize what they want to say over acknowledging someone else.

If someone raises an eyebrow, does a double take, or staggers back at something you've said—will you break your stride to acknowledge it? Good conversationalists absolutely will because they can feel the flow of the conversation. It doesn't matter if you didn't finish your story or wanted to speak more on the topic—don't sacrifice the opportunity for a valuable exchange of ideas just to keep your conversation linear and neat.

When you don't acknowledge, you're treating your conversation more like a lecture or a speech. *Please hold all questions for the end.* The whole point is to make people feel like they matter to you and aren't just some anonymous or convenient audience to your soliloquy.

When you regularly start being mindful of acknowledgments, you might recognize patterns in your life—people who never acknowledge, people who always acknowledge, and people who only like to hear the sound of their own voice. There are also those that are relatively shy and confrontation-averse. When you interrupt them, start speaking simultaneously, speak over them, or in any way do not acknowledge them, they may not care or care to raise the issue, and are all too happy to let you drone on.

You will help them out tremendously by apologizing and acknowledging that they were about to speak and you interrupted. They'll be thrilled. They don't want to interrupt you, so if you take the burden yourself, they'll feel validated and heard. One example is to say, "Oh wait, just a moment, what was it you were about to say?" or "Sorry, what were you going to say? You seemed like you had a reaction to that!"

Make sure that when you get a reaction, you quickly acknowledge and ask a follow-up question. Don't give in to the temptation of continuing with what you have to say. What you have to say is not as important as the level of mutuality and understanding you're creating by effectively conversing with the person in front of you.

People like to be heard. They feel good when they are acknowledged, validated, and accepted. When people say things, they don't want just silence. They want to be made to feel that whatever they have to say matters.

Enough Is Enough

I had the distinct displeasure of sitting through a speech recently where the speaker was obviously pumping with adrenaline and fatigued simultaneously. That's what nerves can do to some people.

He kept messing up his wording and pronouncing things incorrectly. Whenever he did this, he digressed for about 5–10 seconds while he went back to explain what he did, why he did it, and overcorrect himself. Then he vacillated as to the choices he could have made and the choice he ultimately went with. In the end, there was far too much detail about vocabulary and the technical requirements of a PowerPoint presentation in his talk about leadership techniques.

It was incredibly unnecessary and exhausting to listen to. But there was a valuable lesson in his shortcomings.

First, what is your main message? Second, how do your corrections relate to the main message? Third, does anyone care about your correction, or is it just for you?

Sometimes we want to convey something, but the overall message gets lost because we get bogged down in unnecessary details. These are details that no one really cares about—even if they're wrong in a superficial way.

Imagine you are a busy doctor who sees 30 patients in your nine-hour work day. That doesn't leave a lot of time for each patient, and might even explain why your handwriting is so rushed and poor.

You ask your patient what's bothering him. He tells you that he hurt his arm falling off his chair. Then he corrects himself—it's not a chair exactly; it can also be used as an outdoor recliner—by the pool—he thinks it's made of fiberglass … but he really needs to check the manual for that. Oh, and now he wonders if he left his kitchen stove on, but oh, he really loves that chair and he thinks it might currently be on sale.

As his doctor, do you care about any of this? Absolutely not.

The same kind of dialogue plays out in daily life. Serious fat in the form of unnecessary overcorrection can be trimmed from many conversations. The overcorrection only serves as an external dialogue for you and detracts from the overall point of your message, making it ambiguous. I know I made the point earlier about thinking out loud more—but only when it's substantive and not when it's meandering thought.

For example, suppose you are showing someone your kitchen and you don't use your dishwasher because you use it for storage. You could just say that you're using it for storage and leave it. But instead, you go on to explain that you use it for storage but not always. Sometimes you use it to wash dishes, but only if there are a lot of people over. Sometimes there's a drought and you feel like saving water. And other times, you are feeling lazy and you use it, just like that one time you were sick. But then again, water is important.

What was the point again?

Just cut straight to the chase. Cut the clutter. Get rid of unnecessary details and focus on the overall point. This may not seem like a big deal, but again, it's the cumulative effect that creates and impression and influences how you're perceived by others. You'll be seen as the unfocused person who tells terrible stories and can't stay on topic even if your life (or theirs) depends on it.

Don't let the details and corrections drag you away from the story you mean to tell. Leave them and get to the point! They don't add any value to what you're saying—you're just debating with yourself out loud. There is no quiz for accuracy after you tell a story.

This is easy to talk about but it's hard to put into practice because sometimes the details that impact us don't really matter to others. For instance, in a story about hiking, or how pretty a particular rock was. This detail doesn't make the story more vivid for anyone but you. Be clear about what the focus is and try not to stray from it. Details don't make a story shine; the inherent emotions do.

Simplicity and not overcorrecting or backtracking makes your stories more captivating. It also prevents confusion and, most importantly, prevents you from boring people out of their minds.

This also applies when you are the listener. When the speaker offers unnecessary details or points to the story they're sharing, don't indulge them. Gently remind them of the central point of their story. Don't pay attention to their overcorrections. Don't ask minute detailed questions regarding their story to make them feel compelled to correct.

For example, someone is telling you a story about a fire in their neighborhood. If they start wondering out loud about the color of the firetruck, ignore them, and ask them about the actual fire. And if they happen to misspeak, don't correct them; let it slide. And don't ask them about the minutiae of the story. This flies in the face of the overall objective you should have.

Stacking

A final way to keep a conversation flowing effortlessly is to stack onto the information that's given. When you think of the word stacking, you probably imagine the game of

Jenga or some kind of log cabin that Abraham Lincoln was supposedly born in.

That's about the right feeling for this tactic. When you are stacking in conversations, this means you are adding directly to what you have just heard from your conversation partner. Suppose their statement is X, all you have to do is say X + Y, where Y is a new piece of information. You can add any piece of information you want as long as it's somewhat related to X.

One of the easier ways to stack in conversations, if you know the other person well, is to add in common history. All you're doing is referring to something that relates to the first statement that you have experienced together. The good part is that this inevitably brings up fond memories; the bad part is you might have to hunt a bit in your memory banks for something that applies.

Jim: "I went to the football game this weekend."

Bob: "Like the time we went in college and you almost broke your foot?"

Jim: "This juice is great."
Bob: "Remember when we picked apples and you almost broke your foot?"

Jim: "I didn't know she was so nice."
Bob: "Kind of like when you almost broke your foot doing charity when we were younger?"

It seems Jim has a tendency for being clumsy. You can view this as similar to the HPM + SBR chapter in that it's a specific response you can whip out in most instances. This one has a bit more leeway, though, because the main purpose is to simply add information.

The second way you can stack and add information in a conversation is to make small assumptions and ask, "If X is true, then what else is true?" What assumptions can you make based on X being true or being mentioned? What information can I add here? Let's go back to clumsy Jim and Bob.

Jim: "I went to the football game this weekend."
Bob: "Did you get drunk and wear a hat with foam cheese on top?"

Jim: "This juice is great."
Bob: "Is it your favorite juice, or would you rather have a nice mojito?"

Jim: "I didn't know she was so nice."
Bob: "Sounds like you're interested in taking her out to a steak dinner."

All of the examples above simply ask the question, as mentioned, "If X is true, then what else is true? What assumptions can we make?" It doesn't even have to be plausible; it's just meant to facilitate conversation by stacking upon the information someone else has given you.

If you imagine conversational flow as a stream, then falling prey to the problems in this chapter represents boulders that disrupt the stream. A couple might even be flat-out dams that stop the conversation altogether. That's why it's so important to identify the ways you are impeding flow and throwing a wrench into what could be excellent rapport.

Chapter 10: Awkward Situations

What we've had in this book thus far is a compilation of tactics to make you better at conversations flat-out. Some address the phenomena of awkward silences, but what about specific awkward situations that you'll encounter on a daily basis?

The consequences of these situations are far worse than simple awkward silences. Sure, that's how they all begin, but we often find ourselves in situations that can lead to more abrasiveness or tension if we don't know how to properly handle them.

What are these awkward situations to speak of? I would wager you've experienced all of them at some point in your life, at which point you had a few options. First, you might have addressed them with an iron fist out of frustration and annoyance and burned your bridges. Second, you may have addressed it in a lukewarm way that didn't get your point across, meaning you didn't get what you wanted. Third, you may have just left it alone and swept it under the rug because you were so averse to conflict.

None of these outcomes are ideal, so here are a few ways you can change that.

Accidentally Insulting Someone

Suppose you make a faux pas and ask your obese coworker when her baby is due. Now, this is an accidental insult because you had good intentions, but it was poorly delivered and easily misinterpreted. Whatever the case, your positive or neutral message has turned into an insult.

How do you recover from this? Remember, there is no golden method to take back what you said, but these methods can help smooth it over.

First, if you are quick enough, you can slap a "just kidding" onto the end of it and make a joke out of it, albeit a mean joke. This might not be much better, but at least you are turning an insult born out of obliviousness and a lack of self-awareness into something conscious.

"Marie, when is the baby due? I didn't know!" turns into:
"Marie, when is the baby due? I didn't know! Just kidding, bad joke. So anyway ..." And then immediately move onto a new topic. You can also address the fumble head on:
"Marie, when is the baby due? I didn't know! Just kidding, bad joke. I'm such an oblivious person and I'm obviously blind."

Second, you may have unintentionally insulted someone, but you can just as easily turn it into something about yourself. This works at deflecting harm because when people show vulnerability, our instinct is to go easy on them and try to make them feel better about themselves. In other words, make the insult about you, not about them.

"Marie, when is the baby due? I didn't know!" turns into:
"Sorry, I didn't mean that. I've just struggled with weight and body image issues since I was young so sometimes I project that onto others. It doesn't mean anything about you. It's all about me. It all started back when ..."

See how you have subtly turned the tables and sort of insulted yourself to take the negative spotlight?

The third way to deal with accidentally insulting someone is to simply own up to it directly. Admit your mistake and apologize as genuinely as possible, then try to change the topic with a positive spin.

"Marie, when is the baby due? I didn't know!" is followed by:

"I'm sorry. That was really insensitive. I don't even know why I said that. I should have kept my mouth shut. I really love your shoes, though. What brand are they?"

Keep in mind none of these tactics will suddenly make people forget the hurtful thing you may have said, but they help smooth over the aftermath.

Forgotten Names

You know his face and you even know where he works. But you've forgotten his name.

Has this happened to you before? Then you know it feels extremely rude and insensitive to ask for someone's name directly after meeting them once or twice before. It truly gives the impression you don't care about them and they aren't memorable—maybe they aren't, but at least you can keep that under wraps.

What are some ways to covertly discover someone's name without having to ask them for it directly? The first way is to sneak away and ask someone else in the vicinity, but this isn't always possible and there aren't always other people around. Therefore, these methods involve getting the person to say their name for another purpose than to tell you.

First, you can introduce this mystery person to a friend, or anyone else nearby. You don't need to use their name to introduce them, you can just grab both people and say, "Hey, have you two met each other?" and they will naturally introduce themselves and shake hands. You don't even need to remember either person's name for this tactic to work.

Second, you can ask them for their contact information or business card. Insist that you want to keep in touch with them in the future and ask how you can make that happen. If they want to give you their phone number, insist they enter it into your phone so they actually have to type their name in first. If they want to give you their email address, often their name will be in it. Ideally, they give you a business card so you have their full name to refer to.

In the process of getting their contact information, you can also ask them to spell their name for you by claiming that you are terrible with spelling. Even if their name is Kevin or Eric, they will make some mention to it: "You don't know how to spell Kevin?"

Finally, you can always apologize and claim to be a combination of terrible of names, and stressed out on the day you met originally. This is probably answer most close to the honest answer of, "I didn't pay enough attention to you so I forgot." Most people have had days like this, so there is a level of understanding. It almost sounds legitimate!

Escaping Conversations

Sometimes we're stuck in a situation we can't extract ourselves from because we feel too awkward, or we can't find a moment of silence to jam in an excuse. We know we don't like it when others disengage from us abruptly, so we want to be able to do the same without those negative feelings. We just want to be able to escape in a graceful way that doesn't ruffle any feathers.

If you end your social interactions abruptly, you can come off as hostile, socially incompetent, or a bad person. Of course, none of this is true. You just want to get out of there. You have to master the art of *bowing out of conversations* gracefully and heading for the exit. There are a few ways to do so without friction.

First, you can tell others you got a call, text, or email that you need to deal with urgently. Not even your close friends or coworkers know the details of your daily obligations, so it's easy to simply look at your phone and express surprise or concern. Almost no one will have a problem with it because they know that urgent issues pop up all the time. It's perfectly legitimate.

"Excuse me, do you mind if I step out and take this?"

"Sorry, I just got something that looks urgent. Do you mind if I head home to take care of this?"

You can also just glance at your phone to see the time and say something like, "Wow, I didn't realize the time. Do you mind if we continue this later? I have to deal with something on a deadline today."

You don't even have to elaborate much on what you are supposedly dealing with. It might be better to keep it vague so you're not caught in your web of lies later on. The key here is to ask for permission to be excused. It's a gesture of good will. It makes it clear that you are taking the other person into consideration, and being courteous so as to not reject them for something else. Besides, it's not like anyone will refuse permission by saying, "No, stay here and talk. I'm more important than your job."

Second, you can tell others you need to be excused to use the bathroom. Just make this excuse seem urgent, and they'll completely understand it. Again, this is because literally everyone has felt the sting of the growing water balloon inside them when they have to resist going to the bathroom. "Wait, I'm sorry. I've been holding my bladder ever since I got here. Can you excuse me?"

Third, similarly to the bathroom scenario, you can say you need to talk to someone else. This may seem like it would be rude, but people have no problem with this if you do it correctly. The key is to make it seem important and urgent.

If you see someone walking by, you could say, "Oh wait, is that Steve? I'm sorry. I need to catch him, and I've been calling him constantly. Can you excuse me?"

If you're isolated and you don't see anyone walking by, you could say, "I know this is random, but do you think Steve is around? I called him three times and he didn't get back to me. I think I need to check on him. Can you excuse me?"

The three tactics in leaving I mentioned have a few themes in common, which is why I also want to provide a small framework for the most acceptable way to escape an interaction. If you find yourself in a situation where you can invoke all of these factors, you can escape anything.

First, have an excuse ready to leave any conversation or social situation. The bathroom, needing to call someone, or searching for someone else always works. It doesn't have to be too specific; just have something ready on the tip of your tongue.

Second, act as if the need for an exit is urgent so the other people in your context won't take it personally or question it. This is important because we sometimes feel that leaving a conversation is tantamount to rejecting someone. In a way, it is, but we can mask that feeling by conveying urgency and importance. No one is going to feel insulted if you need to go home because your apartment is flooding.

Third, ask for permission and then apologize for having to leave. Drive home how genuine and courteous you are. Show remorse about the fact that you are escaping and they'll feel good about it.

Finally, say something about the future. For example, "Let's do this again soon" or "I want to continue this conversation!" This adds a final level of empathy and care so people can feel good about the fact that you are departing.

As you can see, most of these factors are aimed toward obscuring the fact that you simply don't want to be there anymore, and sparing the feelings of the other people. You are conveying your full message, but without the negative impact.

These four steps can help you build an exit strategy for wherever you go, and whatever situation you find yourself in. Is it deceptive? Some could see it that way, but if the alternative is to get cornered by someone who lacks the self-awareness to see you yawning while you are already exhausted, making you grumpy and annoyed, then I would choose to convey the message without the impact every time.

How to Get Paid Back

Ever been in the situation where you've lent a friend money, but aren't sure when you're actually going to be paid back?

This is why people typically warn against mixing business with pleasure. Money is a dicey topic between humans, and it gets even dicier between friends. It might even be the worst and most complex between family. Is it a gift, a loan, or even expected to be repaid? Is there some familial sense of expectation? Who knows what you might be dealing with in the absence of a business agreement and written contract.

Those certainly aren't practical for everyday situations such as going out to lunch with friends. But suppose you notice you keep paying, and your friend keeps telling you they'll pay you back, but then keeps "forgetting their wallet" or any number of excuses. Even $4 can start to add up and you continually let them off the hook.

First, you can set the terms of the debt by explicitly saying, "Okay, I got the last one. You get this one, right?" Take the pressure off the current moment, and set the terms going forward that they have agreed to. When the time comes, you can say, "I'll get this one. You can get the next!" or "Remember I paid last time. You want to get this one?"

In many ways, this is easier because remembering exact amounts for each item or meal is difficult and feels petty. Therefore, remembering who paid for the most recent "thing" is easier and more manageable. Just make sure to take notes for the occasion, and amount each occasion so the person can't simply say they don't remember whose turn it is—*you do,* and you have the documentation to prove it.

In a sense, you are putting them on the spot with their debt. This can occasionally backfire if they truly don't have the money, so you can take this step before meeting up or agreeing to go out to ensure you aren't left holding the short end of the stick again.

If it's not an ongoing situation and you simply want your money back right now, then it goes back to what we discussed in escaping conversations—you need to create a compelling reason. You need to make up a reason you need the money sooner rather than later, or even immediately. In this case, you aren't necessarily asking for the petty reason that you want $5 back; you are asking because you want or need to put the money toward something important. For instance, "I have to scrounge together some money for an unexpected bill. Can you pay me back today to help me out?" or something with smaller stakes, "I need more cash to pay for my doctor's appointment later today. Do you have the money you owe me?"

Even though people who owe money are technically in the "wrong," they bristle easily if people demand payback. They often take it personally and become defensive. You don't actually need any reason to get your money back other than, "Hey, please pay me back." But it's a tense topic, so being able to blame a reason can help get your money back while also keeping your friendships.

Another way to get your money back, or at least get the same amount of value, is to ask the person to buy you something or perform a service for you, and then deduct what they owe from the end price. For instance, you can ask them to bring you lunch, or ask them to pick you up from the airport. Small things can add up in value, so you don't necessarily need money back even though that's what you lent out.

Your friend may not have the money, but they'll have time and willingness to help out and sometimes that's even better for you. You can address it beforehand, which makes it clear as to your intent and the fact you are keeping track:

"I'm going to be flying in tomorrow night at 9:00 p.m. Think you could pick me up? I'll take it out of what you owe me."

"Do you think you can pick up pizza on the way over? I'll deduct whatever the price is from what you owe me."

Some people still might bristle that you dare to keep a ledger of what's owed to whom— but that's ironic because these are the same people that say it's petty to keep a ledger over $5 while continually avoiding paying you that same $5. Go figure.

The final way to get your money back is to have someone else do it for you. As you may have noticed, you can face significant blocks when demanding money back from people. Namely, you might just be too uncomfortable for that amount of confrontation. That's why asking someone else to do it for you, or gently prompting others, can be so helpful.

It takes you out of the equation and puts a spotlight onto someone's debt as viewed by a third party. When a third party calls you out and asks why you haven't paid someone back yet, you can be sure that will garner greater attention. It might be because of social shame, but whatever works as long as you are kept out of harm's sight. In other words, let someone else be the messenger of an uncomfortable demand while you stand to the side and benefit.

As mentioned, you can instruct people to be as gentle or aggressive as you want—the messenger is a sacrificial lamb and it won't necessarily be traced back to you. You're just the beneficiary.

Gentle: "Hey, don't you owe Patrick some money? What was it, like $500? If that was me, I would pay them back ASAP?"
Medium: "I heard you owe Patrick $500? I'd be so mad at you if you didn't pay me back ASAP."

Aggressive: "When are you paying Patrick back? That's messed up. No excuses."

Overall, combining friends and family with money does not create outcomes you will enjoy. You just might have to accept a loss of around 10% of what you loan or give—call it the "dealing with friends and family" tax, whether through malice, laziness, or apathy.

Awkward situations exist everywhere, but hopefully the common threads in this chapter provide guidance elsewhere.

Conclusion

People place arbitrary barriers around their view of social situations, and they end up living in invisible prisons they create for themselves.

How often have you heard, "You can't say that" or "You're not supposed to ask about that."

Well, why not?

No wonder so many of us are in fear of what to say that it paralyzes us. In other words, no wonder awkward silences are so widespread and common. I like to remind people that it's not necessarily that you've run out of things to say. Your mind still has the monkey chattering about; rather, you just don't feel comfortable blurting out what the monkeys have proposed.

That's the real cause of awkward silence in our everyday lives. This book isn't necessarily about taming the monkeys; it's about giving them a few guidelines to be more productive.

Sincerely,

Patrick King

Social Interaction Specialist and Conversation Coach at
www.PatrickKingConsulting.com

P.S. If you enjoyed this book, please don't be shy and drop me a line, leave a review, or both! I love reading feedback, and reviews are the lifeblood of Kindle books, so they are always welcome and greatly appreciated.

Speaking and Coaching

Imagine going far beyond the contents of this book and dramatically improving the way you interact with the world and the relationships you'll build.

Are you interested in contacting Patrick for:

- A social skills workshop for your workplace
- Speaking engagements on the power of conversation and charisma
- Personalized social skills and conversation coaching

Patrick speaks around the world to help people improve their lives through the power of building relationships with improved social skills. He is a recognized industry expert, bestselling author, and speaker.

To invite Patrick to speak at your next event or to inquire about coaching, get in touch directly through his website's contact form at http://www.PatrickKingConsulting.com/contact, or contact him directly at Patrick@patrickkingconsulting.com.

Cheat Sheet

Chapter 1. You Set the Tone

You have more choices than you might expect when you are engaging with people. Your primary choice is the tone you wish to set. You can treat people like strangers, or like friends. You can speak like strangers, or with child-like wonder. You can attempt to remain intellectual, or speak like a human being. The choice is yours; the tone is yours to set.

Chapter 2. The Devil Is in the Details

Sometimes the smallest things can make the biggest difference, or at least have a startling cumulative effect. Upspeak, the phrasing and vocabulary you tend to use, and catering to people's attention spans all seem like ancillary aspects of charm, but they have great importance.

Chapter 3. HPM + SBR

HPM and SBR represent six different ways you can engage people beyond the generic, boring answers you would normally give. They are history, philosophy, metaphor, specific, broad, and related. HPM draws from within, while SBR draws from the information right in front of you. I suggest experimenting and seeing which resonate the most with you—and then practice those that do not so you have as much in your ammunition box as possible.

Chapter 4. Tell Me a Story

We're always taught how to tell stories, but not how to receive and listen to them. You should phrase questions in a way to ask for stories, strive to keep the spotlight on other people (even in your own stories), occasionally show shock, and beware of know-it-alls and one-uppers.

Chapter 5. The Witty Comeback Machine

Witty comebacks don't necessarily insult back; they deflect in a way that you are able to show your wit and creativity. The formula of agree + amplify is golden. Self-deprecation can also achieve the same effect, but is more useful for disarming others and showing security.

Chapter 6. Conversational Diversity

Conversational diversity must occur in any good conversation. No matter how good you are, you'll still fall into patterns. You can experiment with hypothetical questions, thinking out loud, analogies, and third-party references—all of which give you degrees of unpredictability because you are forcing people (and yourself) to respond to something novel.

Chapter 7. Conversational Diversity Part 2

Additional ways to add a dash of diversity and spice into your conversations include personal and unique compliments, being unpredictable with the way you answer common questions, and mastering the elements of sarcastic remarks and humor.

Chapter 8. Can You Stop That?

We all have bad habits. Most of this book talks about what to do. What about what to avoid? Avoid laughing first on a consistent basis, the elements that lead to creepy behavior, and giving unsolicited advice—it's *always* unsolicited unless they literally ask you for advice.

Chapter 9. Keep It Flowing

Conversational flow is important because it is the antithesis of awkward silence. Easy ways to create flow include engaging on mutual interests instead of self-centered pursuits, taking charge of interruption scenarios, resisting debating and arguing, acknowledging everything, stacking and adding information, and avoiding the tendency to overcorrect.

Chapter 10: Awkward Situations

We encounter awkward situations and make them worse every day. Learn the common guidelines for each of the following: accidentally insulting someone, forgetting someone's name, escaping a terrible conversation, and getting your money back from anyone.

Made in the USA
Columbia, SC
25 January 2019